How To Succeed In Life

Ideas and Principles They Don't Teach In School

Diamond Publishing Company
Shaker Heights, Ohio

How To Succeed In Life

Ideas and Principles They Don't Teach In School

by *Ned Grossman*

In a fast-paced, race-from-one-thing-to-the-next world, Ned Grossman offers inspiring insights and anecdotes on how to live a life filled with success, joy and happiness.

How To Succeed In Life
  Ideas and Principles They Don't Teach In School
Copyright © 1994, 1996 Ned Grossman

Diamond Publishing Company
20600 Chagrin Blvd., Suite 250
Shaker Heights, Ohio 44122-5334
(216) 561-0762, 1-888-WORKHRD (1-888-967-5473)

Marketing & Media Relations: Penhallurick & Associates, Inc.
   Cleveland, Ohio
Cover design: Concialdi Design, Frankfort, Illinois
Text Preparation: Cheryl Broadway

Library of Congress Catalog Card Number: 94-092405

ISBN: 0-9648710-0-9

Printed in the United States of America

Grossman, Ned

Insights and anecdotes on how to live a life filled with success, joy and happiness/by Ned Grossman

        1. Self-help. 2. Motivation. I. Title

A limited first printing of this book was done in October, 1994.
Second Printing November, 1995
Third Printing July, 1996

To Jennifer and Adam

To my two wonderful children, Jennifer and Adam:

When you were born, I had three wishes for you:

♦ To be healthy. Obviously, I have no real control over that. Fortunately you both are healthy and my number one wish has come true.

♦ To become independent. I thought I could help you a little here. Fortunately you both are very independent and my number two wish has come true.

♦ To experience the thrills, excitement and joy of a Championship sports team in Cleveland.

Now that you are teenagers, I thought I should do something more for you than wish for a sports miracle---something important, meaningful, relevant, beneficial. Something that, hopefully, would provide you long-term benefits.

Writing this book has been my attempt to give you a road map to happiness, success and all the things in life you really want. Since you were born, you have heard me preach these ideas. Over the past ten years I have tried to put them on paper to give you a simple, easy to follow, reference guide.

Thank you both for being such wonderful, loving young people and for being the impetus and inspiration for what has been an enjoyable project that has given me fun and pleasure.

I do have one further wish for you. If you decide to have children of your own, may they bring you the same joy, happiness and satisfaction you bring me every day.

CONTENTS

1. An Introduction 1

2. The Two Things Everybody Wants 7

   Happiness 7
   Success 13

3. What We Need to Understand to Achieve
   Happiness and Success 25

   Control and Responsibility are Ours . . . 25
   Opportunity is Everywhere 34

4. Six Rules to Achieve Happiness
   and Success 39

   We Become What We Think About . . . 39
   Decide Exactly What You Want 42
   Determine the Price You Have to Pay . . 44
   Commit to Pay the Price 44
   Work Hard, One Day at a Time 45
   Never Give Up 47

5. Your Most Precious Assets 57

   Your Body 57

       Health 58
       Nutrition 61
       Exercise 65
       Stress Management 69

   Attitude 74
   Time 82

6. Critical Elements for Achievement 91

    Do Your Own Thing 91
    Do Your Best 104
    Goals 107
    Laws 116

7. Topics for Personal Well-Being 119

    Love 119
    Kindness 123
    Life 126
    Feelings 131
    Think and Then, "Just Do It" 133
    Security 139
    People 141
    Friends 146
    Parents/Children 151

        Your Parents 151
        You As A Parent 153
        Your Children 157

    Worry 163
    Fear and Failure 167

8. Attributes to Cultivate 175

    Enthusiasm 175
    Creativity/Imagination 179
    Truth and Honesty 184
    Uncommon Attributes 187

        Character 187
        Courage 188
        Class 189

Common Sense 189

Communicating: Listening and Talking . 191
Self Esteem & Confidence 197

9.   Career 203

Money/Riches/Wealth 203
Work/Business 211

    Excellence and Quality 219
    Service 224
    Customers 227

Uncommon Leaders/Peak Performers . . . 231
Education 236
KISS 243
Luck 245

PREFACE

This is not a typical book. You do not have to start at the beginning and read continuously to the end. You can skip around, pick and choose topics that may be particularly interesting or pertinent.

♦   ♦   ♦   ♦   ♦

There are many quotations at the end of most chapters. They are there for three reasons:

♦   They provide the thoughts and ideas of history's greatest thinkers who were far wiser and more intelligent than I.

♦   They may provide you with one exquisite thought or piece of philosophy that you can grasp, embrace enthusiastically and carry with you forever.

♦   They probably agree with my own thinking!

♦   ♦   ♦   ♦   ♦

Hopefully you will find this book interesting and thought provoking. Read a little at a time. Digest it. Enjoy it.

1

AN INTRODUCTION

Did you ever read about a frog who dreamed of being a king--and then became one? Well, except for the names and a few other changes, if you talk about me, the story's the same one.
NEIL DIAMOND

My professional background is in insurance, having spent more than 25 years as an employee benefits plan consultant and providing tax-deferred savings plans for individuals. I am not a psychiatrist, a psychologist nor a Ph.D. I do not have years of research and experience in social work or counseling. So writing this manual is definitely not in my field of training or expertise.

Unfortunately, after 18-1/2 years of excellent education, I still had no idea of what I really wanted to do with my life. At the age of 25, having worked for an advertising agency and a small manufacturing company, I was frustrated, unhappy and discontent. I was completely confused about what I wanted to do with, and for, the rest of my life.

Fortunately, I was still single and had no major responsibilities. I decided to quit my job and try to determine exactly who I was and what I wanted to do. My former Shaker Heights High School baseball coach, mentor, and "adopted father" Fred Heinlen, handed me Earl Nightingale's audio cassette program, "Lead the Field." Fred suggested that listening to these tapes might help me resolve my dilemma.

I agreed to listen, not because I thought the tapes would be helpful, but solely as a personal favor to my friend. After all, if a set of recorded messages contained all the wisdom that Fred suggested, why didn't everybody know about them? Why wasn't everybody listening to them? The secrets of success, happiness, fame and fortune just couldn't be that simple and that readily available.

How wrong an "educated" person can be! I had been indoctrinated by the formal educational system, but had never been exposed to the practical common sense realities, rules and laws of success, achievement and happiness. Listening to these tapes turned my life around and put me on the road to achieving everything I had always wanted.

For the past 27 years, I have studied inspirational thinkers, psychologists, and philosophers who have spent their lives studying human nature and the reasons for success. I have learned that the secrets of the universe are not secrets at all. The path to success and happiness has already been laid out for us. We do not have to learn the hard way. All we have to do is read and study these proven philosophies.

In my extensive study, I have found that there is much more than "a common thread" in the ideas and philosophies of these inspirational people. There is a solid foundation of thought as strong as that of the largest building. In their own unique ways, they are all talking about the same common sense rules, laws, principles and philosophies. If we are wise enough to expose ourselves to their thinking, and put their ideas into action, these principles will lead us to everything we want.

♦ ♦ ♦ ♦ ♦

There are countless schools in America Each can teach us reading, writing, arithmetic, science, English, foreign language, etc. But I do not know one school that teaches us how to be successful, how to be productive, how to be self-accepting, how to take responsibility for our own actions, how to be happy, how to "do our own thing," how to set goals and establish priorities, how to be persistent, how to have the right mental attitude.

Life is a game. It can be played and won---just like football, basketball, baseball, bridge or chess. Before we start to play any of these games, don't we need to learn, study and know all the rules? Of course. But, unfortunately, most of us spend our entire lifetime playing the Game of Life without ever learning the rules!

If your life is not filled with everything you want, it is not because of circumstances beyond your control. It is because you have not taken the time and put forth the effort to learn the rules.

For most of our lives we have been drilled by our parents, teachers and religious leaders that the rules are:

- Obey your parents.
- Go to school, get good grades, and do not give your teachers a hard time.
- Go to college if you can.
- If you cannot go to college, get a job.
- Bring home a paycheck.
- Get married.
- Raise a family.
- Pay your bills on time.
- Stay out of trouble.
- Dress nicely.
- Follow the Golden Rule.
- Do everything that everybody else expects you to do.

That advice isn't bad. But, is that really all you want? Following those common rules, the best you can hope to be is just like everybody else---average. Do you want to be just average? What about your sense of purpose, your sense of mission as a human being, your sense of accomplishment, and your desire for unique success?

In this manual, I have compiled a set of rules and guidelines that have existed for years. My purpose is to take these basic ideas and put them into simple, straight-forward language, without any fancy, hard to understand, psychological terms or concepts.

Most of these ideas and thoughts are not my own original thoughts. They are my interpretation of the concepts of brilliant thinkers who have spent their lives studying life. This manual is a layman's attempt to communicate a simple clear-cut set of rules you can follow easily, every day, that will allow you to maximize your potential and to enjoy your life to the fullest.

Be smart enough to begin this study as early in your life as possible. This road map shows you how to find out exactly where you want to go, exactly how to get there, and exactly how to be a winner in the game of life. You have the ability and the opportunity to be highly successful. You can succeed if you decide to take responsibility for yourself and if you believe that your success is a matter over which you have complete control.

The rules are very simple. Become familiar with them, study them, follow them, believe in them. Don't ever give up on them. Eventually, you will create all the success you really want.

2

THE TWO THINGS EVERYBODY WANTS - HAPPINESS AND SUCCESS

HAPPINESS

There is no way to happiness; happiness is the way.
WAYNE DYER

Happiness is something that is inside you. Happiness is not something you can arrive at. It is not a station in life. It is a way of traveling.

Happiness does not depend on money, position or power. It depends on the direction in which you are heading. It is the voyage and the adventure along the way that counts, not the arrival itself. It is not how much you have, but how much you enjoy what you have. So make yourself as happy as possible and try to make those whose lives you touch happy too.

♦ ♦ ♦ ♦ ♦

Happiness may be as simple as deciding that you are glad to be alive and should enjoy every day. Have you ever noticed how many people are unable to be happy today because they are waiting for some future event to make them happy? They think they will be happy when they graduate from high school, or when they get married, or when they have a baby, or when they get a raise, or when they go on vacation, or when Aunt Millie dies and leaves them money, or when their kids finally leave home, or when they retire.

People who wait for happiness to come to them in the future probably will not know how to be happy if, and when, they ever get there. They focus so intently on their present troubles and problems, that they do not simply enjoy today. Make up your mind to be happy now, today and every day.

You already possess all the necessary ingredients for happiness. They are yours today simply for the taking. Most of these ingredients are so commonplace that you take them completely for granted. They are your mind, your body, your health, your spouse, your children, your friends, your home, your job, your colleagues at work.

Happiness, like everything else in life, is something that must be learned and practiced if you are to become skilled at it. It is finding your own unique combination of powers and abilities. It is discovering, through experiment and reflection, what course of action will fulfill you most completely.

♦ ♦ ♦ ♦ ♦

Happiness is a state of mind and a regular condition that we can all attain. Abraham Lincoln said that people are about as happy as they make up their minds to be. Happy people have made up their minds that any alternative to happiness doesn't hold much hope or fun.

♦ ♦ ♦ ♦ ♦

Seeking happiness directly usually results in failure. John Stewart Mill said, "Those only are happy that have their minds fixed on some object other than their own happiness; on the happiness of others, on the improvement of mankind, even on some art or pursuit followed not as a means but as itself an ideal end. Aiming thus at something else, they find happiness by the way."

Happiness comes to productive and creative people when they are engaged in work in which they can lose themselves. The happiest people are usually the busiest people. They are those whose business consists of serving others. They love what they are doing and happiness is simply a part of them. If you give of yourself with no thought of receiving anything in return, there is no limit to the abundance you will enjoy.

♦ ♦ ♦ ♦ ♦

It is an integral part of human nature to be dissatisfied, to want more and to want what you do not have at the moment. Discontent comes with being human.

Moments of complete and blissful satisfaction are rare and soon give way to a nagging desire for something else. That is good. This positive discontent keeps us thinking, motivated and active.

◆ ◆ ◆ ◆ ◆

It is imperative to understand that you are completely responsible for your own happiness. You cannot blame your unhappiness on others--the government, "the system," your spouse, your children, or your job. It isn't the situation that makes you happy or unhappy. You make yourself happy or miserable.

You must realize that it is not other people or exterior conditions that upset you. It is your own thoughts. Then you can decide that you have the power to change your thoughts. It is that thought process that allows you to be happy---right now!

SELECTED THOUGHTS ON HAPPINESS

The happiest and most contented people are those who, each day, perform to the best of their ability.
EARL NIGHTINGALE

Make yourself as happy as possible and try to make those happy whose lives come in touch with yours.
But to attempt to right the wrongs and ease the sufferings of the world in general is a waste of effort.
JAMES WELDON JOHNSON

The happiness of life may be greatly increased by small courtesies. *LAURENCE STERNE*

Your success and happiness lie in you. External conditions are the accidents of life, its outer trappings. The great enduring realities are love of service. Resolve to keep happy, and your joy shall form an invisible host against difficulty.
HELEN KELLER

Happiness is inward, and not outward; and so it does not depend on what we have, but on what we are.
HENRY VAN DYKE

Plenty of people miss their share of happiness, not because they never found it, but because they didn't stop to enjoy it. *WILLIAM FEATHER*

The pursuit of happiness is a most ridiculous phrase: If you pursue happiness, you'll never find it.
C. P. SNOW

The happiness of life is made up of minute fractions--the little, soon forgotten charities of a kiss or smile, a kind look, a heartfelt compliment, and the countless infinitesimals of pleasurable and genial feeling. *SAMUEL TAYLOR COLERIDGE*

It is not in doing what you like, but in liking what you do that is the secret of happiness.
JAMES BARRIE

The happiness of your life depends upon the quality of your thoughts. *MARCUS AURELIUS*

To live long and achieve happiness, cultivate the art of radiating happiness. *B.C. FORBES*

11

Happy are those who dream dreams and are ready to
pay the price to make them come true.
LEON J. SUENENS

I have learned to seek my happiness by limiting my
desires, rather than attempting to satisfy them.
JOHN STUART MILL

It is not how much we have, but how much we
enjoy, that makes happiness. *CHARLES SPURGEON*

Happiness is someone to love, something to do, and
something to hope for. *CHINESE PROVERB*

The greatest happiness of life is the conviction that
we are loved, loved for ourselves, or rather loved in
spite of ourselves. *VICTOR HUGO*

He who enjoys doing, and enjoys doing what he has
done, is happy. *GOETHE*

Action does not always bring happiness, but there is
no happiness without it. *BENJAMIN DISRAELI*

Success is getting what you want. Happiness is
wanting what you get. *DAVE GARDNER*

Doing what you like is freedom. Liking what you do
is happiness. *FRANK TYGER*

To be without some of the things you want is an
indispensable part of happiness.
BERTRAND RUSSELL

No man is happy, but by comparison.
THOMAS SHADWELL

SUCCESS

There is only one success: to be able to spend your life in your own way. *CHRISTOPHER MORLEY*

What a beautiful, simple, meaningful thought. If you are doing what you enjoy, what makes you comfortable, what makes you feel good, what makes you happy, then you are successful.

Success does not equate to wealth or status. It has nothing to do with what other people think about you or your actions. Success has only to do with your own opinions of yourself and what you are doing. If you can get to the point where you can take each day that you are alive, enjoy it fully and make your life work on your own terms by cultivating your own sense of purpose and your own sense of accomplishment and fulfillment, what more can you ask for? How much more successful can you be than enjoying your own life?

Henry Thoreau said, "If one advances confidently in the direction of his dreams and endeavors to live the life which he has imagined, he will meet with a success unexpected in common hours." Note carefully the phrase: "In the direction of <u>his</u> dreams"---not your parents' dreams, your spouse's or your friend's dreams, but your own dreams. Live the life which you have imagined. If you are not doing what is right and comfortable for you, how can you expect to "be right"

13

for your parents, your spouse, your kids, your friends, or your colleagues? Trying to put yourself into a mold created by someone else will lead you to nothing but frustration, anxiety, tension, pressure, and failure.

You can not have a sense of purpose and a sense of accomplishment by leading your life to please others. You only achieve internal satisfaction from your own achievements, not from what anyone else thinks. Nothing is more important to you as a human being than having your own daily sense of purpose and mission.

Running guru George Sheehan says, "Success rests with having the courage and endurance and, above all, the will to become the person you are, however peculiar that may be. Then you will be able to say, 'I have found my hero and he is me!'"

We all want to feel special, significant, and important. We cannot do it by living in the past or waiting for the future. It is living today, now, this moment. Give yourself the freedom and the opportunity to enjoy this moment. It is not your money, prestige, power or awards, but your thoughts, feelings and emotions that give you a sense of purpose. Success is what you feel inside and how you evaluate yourself as a human being.

Whatever personal definition you have for success, it is imperative to understand that success is not an accident. It is absolutely predictable and can be earned by anyone. Success begins inside you--it is a state of mind. It is a function of your character and personality. You carry it with you everywhere. It is as much a part of you as your arms, legs, eyes and ears. You must equate yourself with success.

Success is not due to luck or the breaks or circumstances or the environment. Success is a matter of finding yourself and building upon what you find. We can all become successful, if we will build upon our greatest assets, our own natural resources, the powers that lie within us all.

One excellent definition of success is, "Success is the progressive realization of a worthy ideal." This concept means that people working daily to achieve something they consider realistic and worthy are successful. People with dreams in their minds and hearts that they are actively pursuing are successful.

With this very simple definition of success, wouldn't you think that everyone would be successful? Obviously, they are not. Ninety-five percent of us are not successful because we do not know the rules for success. We have no road map, no specific objective, no goals. We are like ships sailing the seas with no specific destination. We just float along and never reach any worthwhile port. People who really achieve greatness create a vision in their own minds of exactly what and who they want to become, and then they steer themselves toward that vision.

Success does not lie in achievement; it lies in striving, reaching, attempting and growing. The only person who can be called a failure is someone who has stopped trying.

♦ ♦ ♦ ♦ ♦

If you want to be successful, you must learn proven success methods and techniques. One method is the law of attraction which says that whatever thoughts dominate your thinking, you will attract people and circumstances with similar ideas. Our success, or lack of it, can be influenced by the people with whom we associate. If you associate with positive, successful people, you will pattern your actions accordingly.

Success is a matter of habit. We can develop successful habits, live them daily and master them. We can learn how and why other people have become successful and then adopt their habits and philosophies for ourselves. If there is a short-cut to success, it is to learn from others. Do not waste time re-inventing the wheel. Examine the life and behavior of everyone you encounter. Emulate the good. Reject the bad.

♦ ♦ ♦ ♦ ♦

Success is definable and predictable. Learning success is no different than learning cooking, engineering, knitting or golf. You must learn and know what success is and then: JUST DO IT! Become an expert at success. Take courses and seminars. Read books and, easiest of all, listen to tapes.

♦ ♦ ♦ ♦ ♦

Success frequently requires the discipline to delay short-term gratification in order to enjoy greater long-term rewards. Unfortunately, the natural human tendency is to get the things we want now, without concern for the long-term consequences of our short-term actions.

♦ ♦ ♦ ♦ ♦

There are two general groupings of successful people. The first group is "river" people. They have found an activity or a career that has fascinated them and have thrown themselves into it with passion, exuberance and abandon. They work and play in this "river" of interest and love every minute of it. Their work is play and their play is work. Life is a continual joy, a bundle of happiness. Because they love what they are doing, they do it easily, enthusiastically and successfully.

What is your "river" of interest? What do you enjoy doing more than anything else? What can you see yourself becoming "the best" at? You do most often, and with the greatest ease, what you enjoy. If you do not like what you are doing enough to want to be the best, you should start doing something that you absolutely love. Life is too short to waste it doing something you do not enjoy.

The second group of successful people is goal-oriented. They are happy doing many different things. Attaining their goals is important to them. They make up their minds what they want and keep their eyes and enthusiasm on those goals until they become reality.

They enjoy life best by wrapping up one goal and starting right on the next one.

For best results, try to find your "river" of interest <u>and</u> become goal-oriented. Can you imagine a more unbeatable combination?

♦ ♦ ♦ ♦ ♦

Success is a matter of complete mental fitness. It is a euphoric feeling of self-confidence, happiness, enthusiasm and a positive mental attitude that allows us to exist in our world and simply be the human being that <u>we</u> want to be.

Wouldn't it be great to look into the mirror every morning and say to yourself:

- ♦ I am the best person I can be.
- ♦ I am going to spend today in my own way and enjoy it completely.
- ♦ No one on this planet is going to spoil this day for me.
- ♦ I have found my hero and it is me.

SELECTED THOUGHTS ON SUCCESS

To be nobody but yourself, in a world which is doing
its best, night and day, to make you just like
everybody else, means to fight the greatest battle
there is to fight and never stop fighting.
E.E. CUMMINGS

To laugh often and much; to win the respect of intelligent people and the affection of children, to earn the appreciation of honest critics and endure the betrayal of false friends; to appreciate beauty, to find the best in others, to leave the world a bit better whether by a healthy child, a garden patch, or a redeemed social condition; to know even one life has breathed easier because you have lived. This is to have succeeded. *RALPH WALDO EMERSON*

The talent of success is nothing more than doing what you can do well; and doing well whatever you do, without a thought of fame.
HENRY WADSWORTH LONGFELLOW

Success is many things to many people. But, if you have the courage to be true to yourself, to live up to your potential, to be fair with others, and always look for the good in any situation...then you will have been the best you can be, and there is no greater success than that. *LINDA LEE ELROD*

Let us be thankful for the fools; but for them the rest of us could not succeed. *MARK TWAIN*

Success is finding or making the position that enables you to contribute to the world the greatest services of which you are capable, through the diligent, persevering, resolute cultivation of all the faculties that God has endowed you with, and doing it all with cheerfulness, scorning to allow difficulties or defeats to drive you to pessimism or despair. *B.C. FORBES*

Success comes to those who become
success conscious. *NAPOLEON HILL*

Success is a journey---not a destination.
H. TOM COLLARD

When we are young---and some of us never get over
it---we are apt to think that applause,
conspicuousness and fame constitute success. These
things don't. They are only the trappings, the
trimmings of success. Success itself is work, the
achievement that evokes these manifestations. Not the
prize, but that which enters into the winning of it is
what constitutes success. Concentrate on your work
and the applause will take care of itself.
B.C. FORBES

Success consists of a series of little daily victories.
LADDIE F. HUTAR

Both success and failure are largely the results of
habit. *NAPOLEON HILL*

Success is the privilege of doing what you want to
do, when you want, and as you want.
WILLIAM FEATHER

If we are willing to put the best of ourselves in our
present jobs, and are willing to grow slowly,
success will come. *WILLIAM FEATHER*

In helping others to succeed, we ensure
our own success. *WILLIAM FEATHER*

Every outstanding success is built on the ability to do better than good enough. *WILLIAM FEATHER*

Success is simple. Do what's right, the right way, at the right time. *ARNOLD GLASGOW*

You can get everything in life you want if you'll just help enough other people get what they want.
ZIG ZIGLAR

Faith in your own powers and confidence in your individual methods are essential to success.
RODERICK STEVENS

Experience shows that success is due less to ability than to zeal. The winner is he who gives himself to his work, body and soul. *CHARLES BUXTON*

A purpose is the eternal condition of success.
THEODORE MUNGER

Success, as I see it, is a result, not a goal.
GUSTAVE FLAUBERT

Success seems to be largely a matter of hanging on after others have let go. *WILLIAM FEATHER*

The best place to succeed is where you are with what you have. *CHARLES M. SCHWAB*

My belief is that success involves fulfilling one's potential to the maximum. Success is an ongoing process. *MARY CUNNINGHAM*

21

The way you enjoy life best is to wrap up one goal
and start right on the next one. *JIM ROHN*

No student ever attains very eminent success by
simply doing what is required of him; it is the
amount and excellence of what is over and above the
required, that determines the greatness of ultimate
distinction. *CHARLES KENDALL ADAMS*

I know the price of success---dedication, hard work
and an unremitting devotion to the things you want
to see happen. *FRANK LLOYD WRIGHT*

The so-called secret of the really successful people is
treating the people with whom they come in contact
as they themselves would like to be treated if the
positions were reversed. It is so simple, as a matter
of fact, that it is completely overlooked by the great
majority of people. *HENRY FORD*

Six essential qualities that are the key to success:
sincerity, personal integrity, humility, courtesy,
wisdom, charity. *WILLIAM MENNINGER*

Yesterday's formula for success is tomorrow's
recipe for failure. *ARNOLD GLASGOW*

In achieving success, backbone is more important
than wishbone. *FRANK TYGER*

Success comes to those who know it isn't coming to
them and who go out to get it. *FRANK TYGER*

Success is not searching for you. You must
do the seeking. *FRANK TYGER*

The ladder of success doesn't care who climbs it.
FRANK TYGER

Success often comes from not knowing
your limitations. *FRANK TYGER*

The men who succeed are the efficient few. They are
the few who have the ambition and the willpower to
develop themselves. *HERBERT CASSON*

The man who has not struggled with difficulty after
difficulty cannot know the joy of genuine success.
Face them and fight your way over them. There is
more satisfaction in putting forth effort than in
floating over easily won profits. The rungs in the
ladder of success are composed of difficulties.
B.C. FORBES

Success is the reward for accomplishment.
HARRY F. BANKS

To succeed, one must possess an effective
combination of ability, ambition, courage, drive, hard
work, integrity and loyalty. *HARRY F. BANKS*

Success is getting what you want. Happiness is
wanting what you get. *DAVE GARDNER*

Success depends upon doing well with what you can
do well, and not doing what you can't do.
ROBERT HALF

3

WHAT WE NEED TO UNDERSTAND TO ACHIEVE HAPPINESS AND SUCCESS

CONTROL AND RESPONSIBILITY ARE OURS

You should accept absolute responsibility for your life and your success because, as you know, it is not luck, fate, the stars, heredity, circumstances, the economy, the weather, your spouse, your parents or your boss. It is you. You are responsible for what you are and what you will become. To many people, that's threatening. But the truth is, we're all self-made, even though only the successful will admit it.
JOEL WELDON

The great majority of people grossly underestimate their capacity to think, act, determine and shape their own futures. Unfortunately, most people still believe their lives are determined by chance, fate and circumstances. They have not learned that everything in our lives is governed by law and not by luck. We reap the harvest that we ourselves have sown.

We must accept 100% responsibility for our lives---our success, our mediocrity, or our failure. We determine our own life. We make our own choices. We are free to choose our own direction. We must believe that our future is solely and completely within our own hands. Our success is determined by our choices, our dedication, our determination, our will, our persistence and not by accidents of fate or luck.

You can take responsibility for your awareness, attitude, creativity, values, goals, focus, time, sense of humor, commitment, enthusiasm, persistence, preparation, determination, honesty, loyalty, knowledge and service.

Once you accept absolute responsibility for your circumstances, those circumstances begin to improve. Eliminate excuses. Decide what kind of experiences you want to have. Become accountable to yourself. You will find yourself becoming more persistent, more courageous and more determined.

Ultimately, you are the one who is responsible for you. Everything you are or ever will be is up to you. You are the master of your own fate, the architect of your own destiny. Success and happiness begin by accepting total responsibility for your life, for everything that happens to you.

People place responsibility for the events in their lives either within themselves, internally, or outside of them, externally. Losers tend to be external, placing responsibility on somebody else. Sadly, they actually believe someone else is responsible for their fate.

On the other hand, winners tend to be highly internal. They have an almost irrational belief in their own ability to control events, to make things happen. And because they believe that, they actively make things happen because they know they are in control of their own destiny.

Winners discipline themselves to keep their minds calm, clear and balanced. They do not blame others. Losers never accept responsibility; winners always do. When things go well for losers, they attribute it to luck. When things go poorly, they blame it on "the system." Winners take both the credit and the blame for what happens to them. They are always making progress. Winners look to the future. Losers look to the past.

Winners take responsibility for what happens to them. Losers make excuses and blame someone else or something else. If you stop blaming other people, most of your negative emotions will go away. In order to stop blaming, you must accept responsibility.

We all make mistakes. Mistakes are natural and acceptable. No one is perfect. But we must understand that we are not losers---until we blame others for our mistakes. The more we stand up and accept willingly the blame for what went wrong, the more we will respect ourselves and the more other people will respect us. We must take responsibility for our errors and mistakes, learn from them and become better people because of them.

We all have problems, but happy, successful people have a positive attitude toward their problems. They regard their problems as opportunities for challenge, growth and development. When things go wrong, they do not complain about the way the world is. They do not blame other people. They seize a learning opportunity. They ask themselves, "What can I do? What have I overlooked? Where have I miscalculated? What can I do to correct and improve this particular situation?" Successful people do not waste time sulking over their fate. They do not wait for someone else (or God!) to solve their problems. They aggressively look for solutions, options and actions that they can take immediately.

♦ ♦ ♦ ♦ ♦

Our futures are solely and completely within our own hands. We have choices. We decide. We determine our own lives. Whatever we have inside us is not the result of what anybody else put there. We are the sum total of the choices we make in our lives. We cannot always control what goes on outside of us, but we can always control what goes on in our heads. We can control our thoughts and manage our emotions.

We choose everything that goes on inside us. If we do not like something about ourselves, we have the choice of changing it. Understand completely that your life is nothing more than the series of choices you have made, you are making and you will continue to make.

No one else can live your life for you. No one else can make your decisions. The slogan of the happy, successful person is, "If it's to be, it's up to me." We feel good about ourselves to the degree that we are in complete control of our own lives.

♦ ♦ ♦ ♦ ♦

There is a wonderful story of the preacher who was driving by a beautiful farm. The crops were flourishing, having been neatly planted and cared for. The fences, the house, and the barns were freshly painted, neat and clean. Beautiful trees and flowers were everywhere. The preacher hailed the farmer and said, "God has blessed you with a beautiful farm." The farmer paused, thought a moment and replied, "Yes, he has. And I'm grateful. But you should have seen it when he had it all to himself."

The farmer understood that, yes, God had given him a fertile plot with great potential. But, it was the farmer's choice, and subsequent hard work, that had turned the untended raw land into a magnificent farm.

Successful people place no limits on their capacities for living, for contributing and for enjoying their own lives. Everyone, not just a chosen few, can reach the highest levels if they make the choice. The solutions to our problems are simple---taking complete control of our lives and our thinking and putting 100% responsibility for happiness directly where it belongs---on ourselves.

You can do it. You can take charge. You can start thinking positively. You can stop making excuses. You can stop blaming others. You do not have to lie on a couch for 10 or 15 years at $100 an hour. You can say, "I am old enough to realize that what I want, I can achieve. Nobody can change my attitude, my thinking and my behavior but me." Then, really get serious and commit to making the changes you have decided are necessary.

Henry Ford said, "If you don't like the way things are, change them." It is phenomenal what you can do. But you must completely understand that everything that will ever happen to you is up to you.

SELECTED THOUGHTS ON RESPONSIBILITY

Every human being is responsible for himself and not under obligation to meet the expectations of others.
FRITZ PERLS

It's not the situation that makes the person.
It's the person that makes the situation.
HOWARD STEINDLER

People are always blaming their circumstances for what they are. I don't believe in circumstances. The people who get on in this world are the people who get up and look for the circumstances they want. And if they can't find them, they make them.
GEORGE BERNARD SHAW

Your future depends on many things, but mostly on you. *FRANK TYGER*

The price of greatness is responsibility.
WINSTON CHURCHILL

Your success depends upon you. You have to steer
your own course. You have to do your own thinking.
You must make your own decision. You have to
solve your own problems. Your character is your
handiwork. You have to write your own record. You
have to build your own monument---or dig your own
pit. Which are you doing? *B.C. FORBES*

You have absolute control over but one thing, and
that is your thoughts. If you fail to control your own
mind, you may be sure you will control nothing else.
NAPOLEON HILL

We can let circumstances rule us, or we can take
charge and rule our lives from within.
EARL NIGHTINGALE

I have come to the point where, if I am despairing,
I recognize that I have selected despair; and
therefore, I am responsible for my despair.
And if I'm joyful, I'm also responsible for my joy,
and I can celebrate it. So...I put myself in a
position of being fully responsible for me and the
wonderful thing about that is that it frees you
because you have no responsibility. I can't blame
you; I can't blame God; I can't blame anybody.
I can only assume full responsibility for my own
behavior, my own despair, my own tears, my own
joy and, I hope, my own rapture. *ANONYMOUS*

My own view of history is that human beings do have genuine freedom to make choices. Our destiny is not predetermined for us; we determine it for ourselves. *ARNOLD TOYNBEE*

You have been given a road map which, if followed, will keep you on that road. If you neglect to make the start, or stop before you arrive, no one will be to blame, but you. This responsibility is yours.
NAPOLEON HILL

Hold yourself responsible for a higher standard than anybody else expects of you.
HENRY WARD BEECHER

The real freedom of any individual can always be measured by the amount of responsibility which he must assume for his own welfare and security.
ROBERT WELCH

Don't expect to grow if you shrink from responsibility. *ARNOLD GLASGOW*

Man is fully responsible for his nature and his choices. *JEAN-PAUL SARTRE*

There's nothing you can do about the past. But you can do a great deal about your future. You don't have to be the same person you were yesterday. You can make changes in your life---absolutely startling changes---in a fairly short time. You can make changes you can't even conceive of now, if you give yourself a chance. *JIM ROHN*

There's one boss in your life and that's you. The person looking back in the mirror is the one you have to answer to. *WAYNE DYER*

Destiny is not a matter of chance, it's a matter of choice. It is not a thing to be waited for; it's a thing to be achieved. *WILLIAM JENNINGS BRYAN*

When a winner makes a mistake, he says, "I was wrong;" When a loser makes a mistake, he says, "It wasn't my fault." *PAT WILLIAMS*

You have a choice. You can select joy over despair; you can select happiness over tears; you can select action over apathy; you can select growth over stagnation. And it's time that people tell you you're not at the mercy of forces greater than yourself. You indeed are the greatest force, for you. No, you can't do it for me, but you can do it for you.
LEO BUSCAGLIA

To the degree that we concentrate our efforts we will succeed in getting what we want out of life. The ability to concentrate has enabled many people of modest capabilities to reach heights of success that have often eluded geniuses. *MICHAEL LE BOEUF*

Patience is not a virtue if you sit back and wait for your problem to solve itself.
ROBERT H. SCHULLER

If you want to solve your problem, don't wait for somebody else to help you. Tackle it yourself.
ROBERT H. SCHULLER

OPPORTUNITY IS EVERYWHERE

A wise man will make more opportunity
than he finds. *FRANCIS BACON*

The world gives each of us all the opportunity for
fame, fortune, wealth, happiness, success, and security
that we want. Every day, each of us walks by more
opportunity than we could ever develop in a lifetime.
What we fail to understand is that as abundant as
opportunity is, it is also the master of the art of
camouflage. Opportunity doesn't have a huge sign
attached to it saying "OPPORTUNITY." It is discreetly
hidden.

More often we find opportunity right after misfortune,
rather than when we're riding the crest of success. We
have to be intelligent enough to examine every
situation and ask ourselves, "What is this particular
situation trying to teach me? What is positive here?
What opportunity exists?"

Russell Herman Conwell, the founder of Temple
University, travelled the country telling the classic story
of "Acres of Diamonds." An African farmer heard
about people who had made huge fortunes by
discovering diamond mines. The farmer wanted to be
rich, so he sold his farm and began to search the
African continent for diamonds. He spent the rest of his
life in fruitless pursuit of the diamonds that would
bring him wealth. Eventually broke, despondent, and
desperate, he threw himself into a river and drowned.

Meanwhile, one day, the man who had bought the farm, found a large stone in the stream that transversed the property. The stone turned out to be an enormously valuable diamond. He soon discovered that his farm was covered with diamonds. The farm became one of the world's richest diamond mines. The first farmer had owned, literally, "acres of diamonds" but had sold them for practically nothing in order to look for them elsewhere.

Most people seem to feel that the opportunities are always greater elsewhere---in another company, in another town, in another line of work. But before leaving your present pasture, examine it carefully. Each of us is standing, right now, in the middle of our own "acres of diamonds." We need the wisdom and patience to look intelligently at our present situations. We will find they contain the riches we seek--financial, intangible or both. Before we seek "greener pastures," let's be sure our own is not just as green--or even greener. If someone else's pasture looks greener, perhaps it is because it is getting better care.

Spend the time and effort necessary to become outstanding at what you are doing now. There is no such thing as a job that cannot, with time and thought, lead to greatness. If you cannot become outstanding at what you are doing right now, why would you think you could become great at something else? Somewhere in your present job there is an opportunity which can bring you everything you can possibly want. It will not be labeled "OPPORTUNITY." It will be hidden. You've got to find it.

SELECTED THOUGHTS ON OPPORTUNITY

The secret of success in life is for a man to be
ready for his opportunity when it comes.
BENJAMIN DISRAELI

Security isn't what the wise person looks for;
it's opportunity. *EARL NIGHTINGALE*

Believe that every time one door closes, two open.
SCOTTISH PROVERB

Small opportunities are often the beginning
of great enterprises. *DEMOSTHENES*

There is no security on this earth; there is only
opportunity. *DOUGLAS McARTHUR*

Every little event in every day is an opportunity
to symbolize your concerns about the things of
strategic significance to you. Treat every one of
those thousand opportunities as an absolutely
precious moment. *THOMAS J. PETERS*

Opportunity for distinction lies in doing ordinary
things well and not in erratically striving to perform
grandstand plays. *WILLIAM FEATHER*

Difficulties mastered are opportunities won.
WINSTON CHURCHILL

Opportunity can be spelled with four letters. But
these letters are not L-U-C-K. They are W-O-R-K.
B.C. FORBES

Ignorance is blind. The blind cannot see opportunity. Fit yourself to see opportunity. Knowledge illuminates. Mediocre men wait for opportunity to come to them. Strong, able, alert men go after opportunity. Opportunity can benefit no man who has not fitted himself to seize it and use it. Opportunity woos the worthy, shuns the unworthy. Prepare yourself to grasp opportunity and opportunity is likely to come your way. It is not so fickle, capricious and unreasoning as some complain.
B.C. FORBES

The greatest achievement of the human spirit is to live up to one's opportunities and make the most of one's resources. *VAUVENARGUES*

Our real blessings often appear to us in the shape of pains, losses and disappointments; but let us have patience, and we soon shall see them in their proper figures. *ADDISON*

I will study and prepare myself and someday my chance will come. *ABRAHAM LINCOLN*

An optimist sees an opportunity in every calamity; a pessimist sees a calamity in every opportunity.
WINSTON CHURCHILL

Unless a man has trained himself for his chance, the chance will only make him ridiculous.
J. O. MATHEWS

Our opportunities to do good are our talents.
COTTON MATHER

4

SIX RULES TO ACHIEVE HAPPINESS AND SUCCESS

WE BECOME WHAT WE THINK ABOUT

Earl Nightingale, after 30 years of research and study determined the "secret" of success is simply: "We become what we think about."

Success is a matter of expectation. It is amazing how our thoughts, feelings and attitudes at the beginning of a project, game or idea influence the outcome. If we expect to do well on a test, we do. If we expect to enjoy the play, we do. If we expect to play tennis well, we do. No one wins all the time, but people who expect to win, do win more often than people who expect to lose. Positive thinking people seem to get that intangible edge that we often call "the breaks." They expect to succeed just as they expect the sun to rise in the east. They create a habitual attitude and expectation of success.

♦ ♦ ♦ ♦ ♦

We must understand that, first, we must become that which we seek. Whatever we are looking for must first be found within us, whether it be success, happiness, peace of mind or riches. If you don't like yourself and/or the way you are being treated by the world, change into the kind of person you would really like to be. Your world will soon change to reflect the new, emerging you. Before you can achieve the kind of life you want, you must first become that kind of person. You are charged with the cause. The effects will take care of themselves. It never fails.

Why? Because everything operates on the law of cause and effect: good cause, good effect; bad cause, bad effect. You hold the keys. You can change and become anyone or anything you want. Think and act exactly like the person you would like to become. Create a mental image of the person you want to become and act as that person would act in everything you do. Gradually, imperceptibly, you will actually become that person.

There is an inexplicable, undefinable force---call it what you will---that seems to come to the aid of those who develop this healthy attitude and philosophy about positive thinking. People call it "luck," but that is not it at all! It is a force, a momentum, a synchronicity, a serendipity that seems to smile on us.

There are two kinds of people in the world---those who are part of the problem and those who are part of the solution. Which one are you? Each of us makes our own choice---problem person or solution person. It is not what happens to you that makes the difference. It is how you react to each circumstance you encounter that determines your success.

The happiest people are not people without problems. They are people who have learned how to solve their problems. You can alter dramatically the pattern of your life by altering just slightly the pattern of your thinking. You can decide to change from a problem person to a solution person; from a negative thinker to a positive thinker.

When things look bleak, you become sad, depressed, upset, uncertain, negative. But remember, you can change your thinking. We are the only creatures on earth with that powerful ability. Dwelling on the negative only has a negative influence on our lives. Conversely, the more positively you think, talk and act, the brighter, happier and more successful your life will become.

Because you absolutely become what you think about, achieving outstanding success at anything is all a matter of positive thinking. Just make up your mind, once and for all, and then stay with it until you finally accomplish what you made up your mind to achieve. If you think, "I will" and commit yourself absolutely to this philosophy, you can achieve any success you choose.

SELECTED THOUGHTS ON
WE BECOME WHAT WE THINK ABOUT

We become what we choose to become,
whether or not we realize it. *ANONYMOUS*

Make sure your dreams are the greatest influence on
your daily decisions and activities. You will face the
future with anticipation when you have planned a
future you can get excited about, when you have
designed your future results in advance. The future
does not get better by hope; it gets better by plan.
JIM ROHN

We are constantly becoming what eventually
we are going to be. *SAMUEL JOHNSON*

Things turn out best for the people who make the
best of the way things turn out. *JOHN WOODEN*

DECIDE EXACTLY WHAT YOU WANT

We just learned the gospel: "We become what we think
about." We all become exactly what we make up our
minds to become: good or bad; rich or poor; happy or
sad; highly successful or just average. So, what exactly
do you want?

All people who achieve exactly what they want in life
are intensely goal oriented. They have a sense of
purpose, a mission that they must and will accomplish.
They are dedicated to what they are doing, clearly
focused on the vision of the person they want to
become and the goals they want to accomplish.

Discover that wonderful sense of purpose. Most outstanding successes are the reflections of an intense inner fire. Knowing why we want what we want makes the difference between success and failure, joy and frustration. The keys are focus and concentration. To the degree we focus and concentrate our efforts, we will succeed in getting what we want out of life. The ability to focus and concentrate has enabled many people of modest capabilities to reach heights of success that often elude geniuses.

It is imperative to focus your attention and efforts in areas over which you have input, impact and control. Focus on your school grades, your tennis game, your interpersonal relationships, because through hard work, intense effort and determined persistence, you can, to a great degree, control the situations and create the outcomes and desires you want and expect.

Conversely, focusing on the weather, the outcome of a professional sporting event, inflation and American foreign policy is basically a waste of time and effort. These topics are interesting, important, provocative and make for good conversation and debate. However, you have absolutely no impact on the results.

Focus on things over which you have control! There is more about setting and achieving goals in a later chapter.

DETERMINE THE PRICE YOU HAVE TO PAY

There are two rules involved here:

- ◆ You always have to pay full price--there are no discounts, shortcuts or bargains.
- ◆ You always have to pay in advance.

For example, if you want to be a doctor, our society requires an extremely lengthy educational regimen through which you must pass; specifically, years of time, extensive education, sophisticated training. Becoming a doctor requires delay of immediate monetary and worldly gratification, time away from family and friends, sleepless nights, and great dedication. But once attained, a doctor generally receives all the spiritual and material successes our society can bestow.

COMMIT TO PAY THE PRICE

Your commitment to becoming an expert must be absolute---no deviations, no excuses. Pay any price. Go any distance. Spend any amount of time, but become the best at what you have decided to do. Discipline yourself. Give your talents plenty of preparation. Only then can you and will you maximize your abilities.

Success basically equates to becoming an expert. Becoming an expert requires a commitment of time and effort and, most probably, money. Think of any expert---teacher, mechanic, musician, athlete, businessman. Was that expertise achieved easily and without expending time, effort and money? Definitely not!

Your commitment, effort and work must come first. The success, rewards and satisfaction will follow. It is what you bring to your job that is important. It is not what the job gives you. You have control--not the job. Success will come from preparation, self-discipline, hard work, proper use of time, courage, perseverance and faith---paying the price.

We have all heard people say, "I would give anything to..." But the truth is they give very little, often nothing, to do things they say they would give anything to do. These people talk, but they fail to make the commitment and pay the price for success. They talk a good game, but they cannot and do not play it!

For example, after a great pianist had finished her recital, an admirer commented, "I would give anything to play as you do." The pianist replied, "No you wouldn't. If you would, you would play probably as well as I do. You'd give anything to play as I do, except time---except the one thing it takes to accomplish what you want. You wouldn't sit and practice, hour after hour, day after day, year after year. So, you see, you really do not mean, 'I would give anything.'"

When you know what you want, and want it badly enough to absolutely commit to its accomplishment, the answers of "how" and "why" will come to you.

WORK HARD, ONE DAY AT A TIME

Some 4,500 years ago, it was written in Sanskrit, "Look well to this one day, for it and it alone is life. In the brief course of this one day lie all the verities and realities of your existence; the pride of growth, the glory of action, the splendor of beauty. Yesterday is only a dream, and tomorrow is but a vision. Yet each day, well lived, makes every yesterday a dream of happiness and each tomorrow a vision of hope. Look well, therefore, to this one day, for it and it alone is life."

Our lifetime consists of years, months, weeks and days. The basic unit is a single day. Try to live successfully, one day at a time. A successful life is nothing more than many successful days strung together. Each successful day becomes a building block with which you create a successful life. You can only live one day at a time. It is what you do with each day that counts. You need only to perform successfully each act of a single day to enjoy a successful life. The happiest and most contented people are those who, each day, perform to the best of their abilities.

One day at a time. It is a wonderful philosophy and it works all the time. It is only when you worry about the yesterdays that are over and the tomorrows that may never come that you create problems for yourself. It is not the experience of today that causes worry. It is the remorse about what happened yesterday and the dread of what tomorrow might bring. Concern yourself only with today. Anyone can fight the battle for just one day.

Successful people go from one success to another by moving from one successful small act to another. Take one thing at a time in its proper order, staying with that one act until it is successfully completed before going on to the next one. You are developing the habit of success. If you follow this simple formula, you can rest assured that you will be successful all your life.

One successful day at a time will carry you over every hurdle. It will solve every problem. It works every time and for every person. William James said, "Let no student worry about the success of his efforts. If you will do each day as best you can the work which is before you, you will wake up one day and find yourself one of the competent ones of your generation. Take each day as it comes in good cheer, knowing that we only have to succeed each day to guarantee a successful future. It is in this way, that rewards are eventually paid."

NEVER GIVE UP

When asked the key to his success, the great British Prime Minister Winston Churchill summed it up in seven words, "Never give up. Never, never give up."

The history of man is the story of turning defeat into victory, failure into success. If what we are doing is right for us, and we know it, and we have made up our minds to succeed at it, we have only to stay with it, minute by minute, hour by hour, day by day, until we have achieved success.

There is in every failure the seed of an equivalent or much greater success. A little more persistence, a little more effort, a little more creative thinking can turn what seemed hopeless failure into glorious success.

There is no failure except in no longer trying. There is no defeat except from within, no really insurmountable barrier except our own inherent weakness of purpose.

Successful people are rarely discouraged. They seldom walk around with their heads down. They have moments of doubt, concern and frustration, but then they come roaring back. Troubles, problems, and adversities make them work harder and accomplish more. Successful people are dreamers who have found their dreams, their aspirations, their ideas too important to remain fantasies. Their patience, perseverance and "never give up" spirit are rewarded.

In almost every successful person's life, there have been times when the task at hand, or even the world itself, looked too dark to face---no job, no money, no inspiration, bills to be paid, a family to support---times when the individual was on the verge of bankruptcy, despair, panic or even suicide. Then, years later, they could look back and realize that what had seemed like certain failure had really been a great opportunity in disguise. They are grateful that they had the perseverance to stick with it and "never give up."

♦ ♦ ♦ ♦ ♦

Every day there are thousands of people who, without realizing they are on the brink of success, give up in failure. It is strange, but as people approach success, a dangerous thing happens: they have a definite tendency to stop doing the very things that have brought them so close to their goals. They change their actions enough so that the successes they seek elude them. Becoming outstanding, getting rich, achieving success are all matters of a "don't give up" attitude. We must make up our minds once and for all---we commit ourselves---and then stay with it until we finally have accomplished what we set out to do.

♦ ♦ ♦ ♦ ♦

Persistence and commitment build mental toughness and the ability to persevere in the face of adversity. No one is immune from everyday problems, but "when the going gets tough, the tough get going." Sometimes you have to perform at your best when you are not in the mood or are not feeling well.

You have a perfectly natural tendency to underestimate your own powers, to feel despair and to take the easy way out, to give up, to quit. That tendency is especially apparent when you are tired. When you are tired, your problems are magnified.

You must face the challenge at hand. Block the hurt, get the sickness out of your head, shape up and get it together because excuses do not count. Nobody cares if you are sick, tired, or upset. You either do the job or you do not. You must win the mental battle. You must force yourself to remain confident, enthusiastic and positive. You must force yourself to work even harder when you are sick, hurt, sad or troubled. That is mental toughness.

♦ ♦ ♦ ♦ ♦

Only a very few exceptional people really make any serious demands of themselves. The great majority of us achieve far below our abilities---and miss the joy these accomplishments would bring---because, at the first sign of fatigue, we sit down, give up and quit. Overcoming fatigue and utilizing our idle reserves can make the difference between simply existing and really living.

Persistence and courage are functions of your belief in yourself. Ultimately, it is your belief in yourself that determines your success in life. Even if you start off with a low level of self-confidence, if you will persist when the going gets rough, you will build your self-confidence. You will build your resilience. You will build that iron resolution that gives you the strength to "keep on keeping on" when everything seems to be falling down around you.

When you are ready to take the easy way out, try remembering this ten pronged philosophy.

- ♦ If it is to be, it is up to me.
- ♦ I am accountable for my actions.
- ♦ I will offer no excuses.
- ♦ I am committed.
- ♦ I am determined.
- ♦ I am disciplined.
- ♦ I am courageous.
- ♦ I am patient.
- ♦ I am persistent.
- ♦ I will not give up.

Stay with it. Commitment. Determination. Discipline. Patience. Persistence. Do not give up. Perhaps the quality that more than any other is responsible for success is the ability to stick to it longer than someone else.

A great career, a great business, a great home, a great family, a great accomplishment of any kind, a great life all come with patience---patience with ourselves, with others and with the world. People credited with all kinds of ability, talent, brains and even genius frequently have nothing more than the courage and determination to keep on keeping on. They have that one insurmountable quality that is worth all the rest put together. They simply will not give up.

As President Calvin Coolidge said, "Nothing in the world can take the place of persistence. Talent will not; nothing is more common than unsuccessful men with talent. Genius will not; unrewarded genius is almost a proverb. Education alone will not; the world is full of educated derelicts. Persistence and determination alone are omnipotent."

What is the most crucial element of success? It is plain hard work, long hours, unrelenting striving and above all, an obsession that allows you to "never give up."

SELECTED THOUGHTS ON "DON'T GIVE UP" (COMMITMENT, PERSISTENCE, PATIENCE, DISCIPLINE)

Success seems to be largely a matter of hanging on after others have let go. *WILLIAM FEATHER*

Our greatest weakness lies in giving up. The most certain way to succeed is to always try just one more time. *THOMAS EDISON*

A man can be as great as he wants to be. If you believe in yourself and have the courage, the determination, the dedication, the competitive drive and if you are willing to sacrifice the little things in life and pay the price for the things that are worthwhile, it can be done. Once a man has made a commitment to a way of life, he puts the greatest strength in the world behind him. It is something we call heart power. Once a man has made this commitment, nothing will stop him short of success. *VINCE LOMBARDI*

Genius is perseverance in disguise. *MIKE NEWLIN*

We must have dreams and never give up on our dreams. *JIM ROHN*

We can do anything we want to do if we stick to it long enough. *HELEN KELLER*

I believe there is a price tag on everything worthwhile, but it is seldom a monetary one. The price is more often one of dedication, deprivation, extra effort, loneliness. Each person decides whether he or she wants to pay the price. If you do, you achieve beyond other people. *JIM MC KAY*

Genius is eternal patience. *MICHELANGELO*

Here is a sketch of Abraham Lincoln's road to the White House:

1831--Failed in business.
1832--Defeated for Legislature.
1833--Second failure in business.
1836--Suffered nervous breakdown.
1838--Defeated for Speaker.
1840--Defeated for Elector.
1843--Defeated for Congress.
1848--Defeated for Congress.
1855--Defeated for Senate.
1856--Defeated for Vice President.
1858--Defeated for Senate.
1860--ELECTED PRESIDENT.

Patience is the companion of wisdom.
SAINT AUGUSTINE

The will to persevere is often the difference between failure and success. *DAVID SARNOFF*

Never underestimate the power of patient persistence.
ARNOLD GLASGOW

You just can't beat the person who never gives up.
BABE RUTH

One great lesson learned from the study of lives of notable men is that patience, perseverance, stick-to-itiveness and unflagging courage are essential qualities. *B.C. FORBES*

DON'T QUIT

When things go wrong, as they sometimes will,
When the road you're trudging seems all uphill,
When the funds are low and the debts are high,
And you want to smile, but you have to sigh,
When care is pressing you down a bit--
Rest if you must, but don't you quit.

Life is queer with its twists and turns,
As every one of us sometimes learns,
And many a person turns about
When they might have won had they stuck it out.

Don't give up though the pace seems slow--
You may succeed with another blow.

Often the struggler has given up
When he might have captured the victor's cup;
And he learned too late when the night came down,
How close he was to the golden crown.

Success is failure turned inside out--
So stick to the fight when you're hardest hit,--
It's when things seem worst that you mustn't quit.
RUDYARD KIPLING

The price of success is perseverance. The price of
failure comes cheaper. *ROBERT HALF*

Nothing worthwhile ever happens quickly and easily.
You achieve only as you are determined to
achieve...and you keep at it until you have achieved.
ROBERT H. LAUER

54

If you have the desire to excel, the discipline required for the hours of practice and hard work will come more easily. There are no overnight successes. It takes time, work and patience.
GEORGE BURNS, III

You never become successful by dreaming. You become successful by working to the best of your ability and having faith in yourself. To reach your goal, three main ingredients are necessary--self-discipline, determination and desire. There will always be dark days, but with this foundation you will be able to face the challenge. *BERNIE PARENT*

Remember, "Rome was not built in a day." Instant success is never possible. Competence results only from sustained, consistent, self-disciplined effort over an extended period of time. *BUD WILKINSON*

Whatever the project, the key ingredients are persistence and determination. These two traits can overcome most every obstacle. *LAMAR HUNT*

Always give a total effort. Pride in oneself and one's ability comes through knowledge and hard work. Self-discipline is the key to harnessing the energy and dedication necessary to succeed. *STAN MIKITA*

You can accomplish anything if you're persistent enough. *CATHY RIGBY MASON*

Success in life is a matter not so much of talent as of concentration and perseverance. *C. W. WENDTE*

Getting rich, or becoming outstanding at anything, is all a matter of attitude. You just make up your mind once and for all--you commit yourself--and then just stay with it until you finally have what you set out to get. *EARL NIGHTINGALE*

We should concentrate on doing with all our might and mind the thing that lies immediately to hand, doing our best hour by hour, day by day.
B.C. FORBES

There is no such thing as a sudden enlightenment. What there is sometimes is the sudden recognition of how much you've changed through long hard work.
CARDINAL NEWMAN

Commitment lets you know that failure is not failure, but an idea on its way to success.
WALLY FAMOUS AMOS

The biggest obstacle between us and our goals is a lack of total commitment. *WALLY FAMOUS AMOS*

5

YOUR MOST PRECIOUS ASSETS

YOUR BODY

You don't have to be sick to get better.
WAYNE DYER

If you were asked to name your most valuable assets, what would you list? Your home, car, stocks, bonds, bank account, spouse, children, job? If you selected any of the above, you would be wrong.

Our most precious asset is our natural, God-given health. It is our minds and bodies---the things that come to us free! These natural assets are almost irreplaceable. If we properly use them we can easily acquire all the tangible assets that we value so highly.

To utilize properly our minds and bodies, we need to develop a Life Plan. We can achieve all we want--- emotionally, physically, financially and tangibly---if we

will only plan for it. Your Life Plan should cover these
areas:

- ♦ Health
- ♦ Exercise
- ♦ Nutrition
- ♦ Stress management

HEALTH

The amazing fact is that most Americans plan for
everything in their lives except their health. Most
people want to be healthy, happy and physically fit, but
they are unwilling to change their lifestyles to
accomplish their goals. We must make time to examine
and analyze our lives. Where am I? Where do I want
to go? How am I progressing? Am I devoting too much
time to work and not enough to rest, exercise,
enjoyment? Is my body weight where I want it? Are
my blood pressure and cholesterol levels where they
should be?

Take care of yourself. Respect your body. It is the only
body you will ever have. If you do not make time in
your life for health and exercise now, then you will be
forced to take time later for illness. The choice is
yours: health now or sickness later. How can there be
a higher priority than the mind and body you always
carry around with you?

If you stick to these sound health habits, the bad ones
will soon fade away. A healthy, enjoyable life requires
constant vigilance. It literally is a matter of survival.

SELECTED THOUGHTS ON HEALTH

He who has health, has hope; and he who has hope
has everything. *ARABIAN PROVERB*

Health is better than wealth. *ENGLISH PROVERB*

Health is worth more than learning.
THOMAS JEFFERSON

Health is the vital principle of bliss.
JAMES THOMPSON

Health is the condition of wisdom, and the
sign is cheerfulness. *RALPH WALDO EMERSON*

Happiness is more a state of health than of wealth.
FRANK TYGER

Health is so necessary to all the duties, as well as
pleasures of life, that the crime of squandering it is
equal to the folly. *SAMUEL JOHNSON*

Sometimes one pays most for the things one
gets for nothing. *ALBERT EINSTEIN*

The people who will really accomplish great things
in life are those who are willing to discipline their
lives, who maintain their health, their vitality, their
efficiency through this process of rigorous
disciplining of what they take into their bodies and
what they do in life. *BOB RICHARDS*

The sound body is the product of the sound mind.
GEORGE BERNARD SHAW

A feeble body weakens the mind.
JEAN-JACQUES ROUSSEAU

Society is changing from institutional help to
self-help--from doctors, hospitals and pharmacists to
exercise, diet and aerobics. *BARRY ASMUS*

People ought to know that nothing is more
remarkable about the human body than its
recuperative drive, if it's given a modicum of respect.
NORMAN COUSINS

The preservation of health is a duty. Few men
seem conscious that there is such a thing as
physical morality. *HERBERT SPENCER*

Money, achievement, fame, success are important,
but they are bought too dearly when acquired at the
cost of health. *B.C. FORBES*

A healthy body is guest-chamber for the soul; a sick
body is a prison. *FRANCIS BACON*

Your attitude sure improves when you feel well.
JOSEPHINE SAWYER

The secret of staying young is to live honestly, eat
slowly, and lie about your age. *LUCILLE BALL*

How old would you be if you didn't know how old
you was? *SATCHEL PAIGE*

There's only one way to avoid getting old, and that is to be young. *GEORGIA PHYSICIAN*

NUTRITION

I am not a nutritionist, but here is what my own common-sense and experience and a little research have taught me:

What to eat:

- ♦ Pure water.
- ♦ Fresh fruits.
- ♦ Fresh vegetables.
- ♦ Whole-grain cereals and breads.
- ♦ Fresh fish and poultry.
- ♦ Light, low-fat dairy products.

What not to eat and/or put into your body:

- ♦ Refined sugar---Lifts you up, then slams you down. Refined white sugar is pure chemical extracted from plants. It has no vitamins, no protein, no fiber, no fat, no useful minerals, no enzymes, no trace elements---in short, no food value whatsoever. Sugar has been implicated in heart disease, obesity, diabetes, tooth decay, kidney failure and blindness. Even as an energy source, despite being loaded with calories, it fails. Too much sugar taken too fast can literally knock you off your feet.

- Salt---Makes you feel heavy and lethargic. Salt bloats you because it retains fluids in your body.
- Red meat---Contains too much fat and slows you down.
- Fat---Clogs up your bodily engine; keeps the blood from getting as much oxygen to the brain as it should have.
- Caffeine---Gives you a rise in energy, excites you, makes you agitated, then it makes you crash.
- Alcohol---Fogs your mind and is addictive.
- Tobacco---Saps your endurance, is addictive and contributes to an early, gruesome death.

Many people resolve to "go on a diet" in an effort to lose weight. The fact is we are always on a diet. Our diet is what we eat---every day. If we eat the right foods in the right amounts at the right time, our weight will take care of itself. It is the law of cause and effect. Give your automobile the prescribed fuel and it will run smoothly and efficiently. Similarly, give your body the right food and it too will run smoothly and efficiently.

Every time you eat, your body breaks down your food into essential elements. Your system literally manufactures you out of the food you eat. "You are what you eat." You should eat foods that make you smarter, give you energy, make you vibrant and help you sleep well at night.

Proper food intake involves conditioning and forming the proper habits---one day at a time. If weight loss is your goal, go at it logically and slowly. Did you ever see anyone lose 10 pounds in one day? No. But, if you eat properly one day at a time, the weight you want to lose will invisibly fade away. You will not see it go or feel it go, but your bathroom scale and favorable comments from your family and friends will confirm that your program works. Maintaining your proper weight requires strict adherence to your nutrition program. Keep reminding yourself that you are not on a narrow, hard-to-follow diet, but you have adopted a new eating philosophy---a new way of life.

You will soon be positive and enthusiastic about your new eating habits. It will be like a new-found religion. Follow these five commandments:

◆ Change your way of eating.
◆ Be conscious of everything you put in your mouth.
◆ Eat right - eat light.
◆ Eat only when you are at the table.
◆ Eat only in reasonable amounts.

Even with these good ideas and the best of intentions, one problem keeps plaguing me: JUNK FOOD. How do you avoid it? Simple. Do not have any in your house. If they are not there, you cannot eat them! Right now, go through your refrigerator, your freezer, your kitchen cupboards and your basement storeroom. Accumulate all the junk food---candy, cookies, ice cream, crackers, soft drinks, sugar cereals, snacks. Give them to a hunger center. You are doing yourself, your spouse, your children, and your friends a tremendous favor. You are improving their lives by having only healthy foods and drinks available.

This drastic action is not to say you should never again have a cookie, a soft drink or an ice cream cone. When those urges become overwhelming, indulge yourself. That is okay once in a while. But you will have to leave your house to satisfy your urge. I find when there is junk food in the house, I am attracted to it like a magnet. It is too tempting and too hard to resist eating the chocolate chip cookies when you walk past them a dozen times between dinner and bedtime. I can resist anything but temptation! Remove all temptations. Remove and eliminate the junk food.

It particularly upsets me to see my kids eating junk food. I think to myself---why would I allow these two wonderful young people to poison themselves? Shouldn't I stop them? Am I really depriving them if there is no junk food around? Emphatically not.

When Adam was seven, he brought me a glass of purified water on the outdoor patio. It was July, 91 degrees and humid. He said, "Dad, I hate it when we go away like to Bermuda or Pennsylvania." I was shocked and said, "Why, Adam?" He said, "Because the water usually tastes terrible---not like the fresh, clean cold water we have here in the big bottles!" Kids are not stupid. We just have to give them proper nutritional exposure, training and opportunity. They will do the rest.

SELECTED THOUGHTS ON NUTRITION

"Watch what you eat" is wasted advice. How can you avoid seeing it? Any look in the mirror, or a look down and you can plainly see that what you eat has gone to waist. *MALCOLM FORBES*

Perhaps no one realizes how important a good diet has been for me. I cannot describe how important it is. You go along for years weighing too much. Then you change your diet, you start feeling good and you don't even mind looking in the mirror. Gradually, you rise to a different physical and mental level. It reflects on all your life, not just on your ability as an athlete. *JACK NICKLAUS*

EXERCISE

Those who do not find time to exercise will have to find time for illness. *EARL OF DERBY*

Do you ignore your tangible assets? Your house, your car, your investments? Definitely not! You paint your house periodically, service your car regularly and clean and polish it even more often. You check your stocks daily. What about your body? Doesn't it demand and deserve daily attention too?

Most people are surprised by how little exercise it takes to keep your mind, heart and body in good shape and how little food is required for good health. Regular daily exercise will:

- Add years to your life.
- Help you feel better.
- Help you manage stress.
- Keep you looking young and fit.

Aren't these results exciting? Aren't they strong incentive to make you want to start a program right now?

Consider these benefits of exercise:

- The body generally works better when it moves regularly: brain function improves; energy and enthusiasm increase; digestion improves; bones grow stronger.
- Exercise is critical for weight loss and for proper weight maintenance.
- Exercise boosts self-esteem. You gain a sense of your body and what it can do. Once you have a healthy body, you will enjoy it, love it and respect it even more than you do already.

Dr. Kenneth Cooper, the internationally recognized cardiologist, has built his reputation and a highly successful clinic on the concept of aerobic exercise. Aerobic means "with air," or "with oxygen." Aerobics refers to exercises that require large amounts of oxygen for prolonged periods. They are endurance exercises. The five most beneficial aerobic exercises are:

- Cross-country skiing
- Swimming
- Jogging or running

- Outdoor cycling
- Walking

If you can find an exercise that is fun and that you look forward to doing, you have it made. You have found a key to keeping your body healthy and fit. Immediately, you will actually feel the benefits, both mentally and physically. And once you get accustomed to what your new, wonderful, healthy, vigorous body feels like, you are less likely to return to your old, sedentary, inactive lifestyle.

Before you begin your exercise program, consult with your doctor. Then talk to an expert, a personal trainer who can work with you, help you get started and continuously guide you along your chosen path. Start slowly. Remember, you are embarking on a new, lifelong journey that will last 10, 20, 30, 40 or more years---it is not a one-time 100 yard dash!

Walking is the simplest, most easily accessible exercise. The only special equipment you need is a proper pair of shoes. You can walk outside or, during bad weather, in a shopping mall. You can walk alone or with a friend. You do not need a racquet, a field, a court, balls, bats, or a team of people. But, you must do three very simple things:

- Start today. Just walk, slowly, to the corner and back.
- Gradually increase your distance a little each day. These increases will not be painful and are hardly noticeable.
- Do it every day, without fail---no excuses!

♦ ♦ ♦ ♦ ♦

What you don't use, you lose. Inactivity is included in all the lists of coronary (heart) risk factors. Inactivity leads to accelerated hardening of the arteries and causes severe negative effects on both your blood pressure and your cholesterol.

♦ ♦ ♦ ♦ ♦

While no exercise or too little exercise is harmful, so is too much exercise. It is important to understand that you do not have to "kill yourself" running 10 miles a day to enjoy exercise and to be physically fit. Remember---the purpose of life is to enjoy it! Ken Cooper says if you run more than three miles a day, more than five days a week, you are doing it for something other than physical fitness.

I have a 57-year-old friend who for years ran eight miles a day in preparation for 26.5 mile marathons. When injuries began to plague him, he sought medical advice. He was told, "Do not run more than 3 miles a day. You get 90% of the benefit of your workout in the first three miles and after six miles, there is absolutely no incremental value." Did he listen? No! Now, several years later, he is unable to run AT ALL. He has had an operation on one knee and needs one on the other knee.

♦ ♦ ♦ ♦ ♦

A proper exercise program is one you start slowly, enjoy daily, gradually build up to recognizably acceptable limits, and maintain. Then you can relax mentally with the knowledge that you are increasing your chances for a long healthy life.

SELECTED THOUGHTS ON EXERCISE

I think good physical conditioning is essential to any occupation. A man who is physically fit performs better at any job. Fatigue makes cowards of us all.
VINCE LOMBARDI

I've prided myself on being in excellent condition--as good as any man in my profession. Now this doesn't come from sitting on your rear end. This comes from hard, hard work. *WILT CHAMBERLAIN*

True enjoyment comes from activity of the mind and exercise of the body; the two are united.
ALEXANDER HUMBOLDT

A person doesn't stop exercising because he gets too old; he gets too old because he stops exercising.
KENNETH COOPER, M.D.

STRESS MANAGEMENT

Stress is believed to be a major contributor to heart disease, cancer, lung ailments, accidents, cirrhosis of the liver and suicide---six of the leading causes of death in the United States.

How can we reduce stress, tension, pressure and anxiety? We need to learn to take a calm, relaxed attitude toward the world and our lives. We need to realize that everything we seriously want will come to us at the proper time. And, if we do not get something we think we want, we will usually discover later that it was not such a good idea, or all that important. Eventually we realize the situation worked out the way it was supposed to.

Socrates said the greatest thing in life is leisure. Leisure does not mean doing nothing nor being indolent or lazy. Leisure does mean being peaceful, relaxed, at ease and doing something we enjoy. Calmness and serenity are the answers. Easy does it. We need to slow down and become more effective.

When we try too hard, our efforts end in failure. When we relax and do not become overly concerned about the results, the results are generally much better. We worry, fret and stew over things that we later discover were not worth worrying about at all. The harder you try to solve a problem, the more confused and anxious you become. Relax, clear your mind, go for a walk, "sleep on it." You will probably return from the walk or awake the next morning with a solution so simple and so obvious, you will not be able to figure out why you had not thought of it before.

♦ ♦ ♦ ♦ ♦

A mentally healthy person lives life to the fullest and a person who lives it fully enjoys good mental health. Mentally healthy people behave consistently in seven important ways:

- They have a positive attitude. They are people who, no matter what the circumstances, find a way to make the best of everything. They see the good in life and have a great time just being alive.

- They are active and productive. They do what they do because they like it and enjoy maximizing their skills and abilities. They do not feel driven to prove themselves to others. They are in charge of their activities; their activities are not in charge of them.

- They recognize and accept their abilities as well as their limitations. They have a reasonably accurate picture of themselves, and they like what they see.

- They are flexible under stress. They can roll with the punches. When faced with problems, they can see alternative solutions and are not threatened by situations that cause others fear and anxiety.

- They recognize and treat other people as the unique individuals they are. They make everyone feel important and esteemed. They are good listeners. They care about how other people feel.

- They give and receive support and nourishment from family and friends. All too often we think only about ways to cram more and more high-pressure work into our

71

daily schedules. We do not think enough about how to devote more time to family and friends. It feels good to have other people share your life and enjoy it with you. Interact with your family and friends. Be together. Talk together. Walk, bicycle, run, swim and live together.

♦   They tend to diversify. They create a well-rounded life style. They have hobbies and many sources of gratification.---sports, recreation, the arts, reading, community service. If for any reason, they lose some sources of gratification, they have others to turn to. Should a problem arise, they are not broken by it, because there is so much more to their lives than just one key area of interest.

♦ ♦ ♦ ♦ ♦

Positive thinking and positive emotions have direct effects on our daily health and well-being. They allow us to influence whether we are going to be sick or healthy. We can literally control the extent to which we allow some infirmities to keep us down.

We all think we are immortal until we get sick. Then we think we are going to die within the hour. We tend to be intimidated by the slightest pain, and the pain escalates because of it. We are taught to feel pain. And we are taught to give in to pain and to swab pain in lotions, analgesics and pills. People reach instinctively for the painkillers---aspirins, barbiturates, codeine, tranquilizers, sleeping pills and dozens of other analgesics or desensitizing drugs.

What is generally not understood is that many of these vaunted painkilling drugs conceal the pain without correcting the underlying condition. They deaden the body mechanism that alerts the brain to the fact that something may be wrong. The body can pay a high price for suppression of pain without regard to its basic cause. The best way to eliminate pain is to eliminate the abuse.

Pain can be a blessing. Pain is the way the human body has of calling our attention to things that need attention. The body is trying to tell us that we may be doing something wrong.

Changing long-time habits is hard. You have the power and you can do it, but do it slowly and easily. Change one habit at a time. People fail in their attempts to make lifestyle changes because they try to make them all at once. Do not quit smoking, stop drinking, change your diet, and start exercising all the same day---unless you really want to experience stress!

Choose one area for change and improvement. Then work at it diligently, one successful day at a time, for 30 days. That is about the time it takes to integrate a new positive behavior into your daily routine. Then select another challenge and repeat the process, one successful day at a time for another 30 days. Each successive challenge reinforces your past successes. Before you know it, you will have become the healthier, happier, calmer, more energetic person you set out to be.

ATTITUDE

The greatest discovery of my generation is that human beings can alter their lives by altering their attitudes of mind. WILLIAM JAMES

Your most valuable assets are your mind and body. Your mental attitude follows closely. Earl Nightingale called attitude "the magic word" that can turn your life around.

You shape your own life and the shape is determined by your attitude--the attitude you hold most of the time. Develop a positive, healthy attitude toward yourself because :

◆   It is your attitude toward yourself that determines your attitude toward others.
◆   It is your attitude toward life which will determine life's attitude toward you.

The world plays no favorites. It is impersonal---it does not care if you succeed or fail; nor does it care if you change or not. Your attitude toward the world only affects you---not the world.

Frequently, without thinking, people will ask me, "How's the world treating you?" I respond emphatically, "Just the way I treat it!" I am usually given a look of, "Is this guy crazy?" But, it is true. There is a very fine line, if any line at all, between what we expect from life and what we get. So act every day toward the world with an attitude calculated to produce the results you want.

People with the best attitudes naturally rise to the top. They expect good things to happen to them. Usually they get what they expect---not through magic, but because they become the kind of people who earn and are worth their good fortune. You must first mentally become the person you want to be. To develop a good attitude, begin conducting yourself as though you already have a good positive attitude.

Successful people have good attitudes. They are convinced that they can accomplish what they set out to accomplish, that achievement is natural and that there is no good reason why they cannot achieve all they want. Successful people expect more good out of life than bad. They expect to succeed more often than they fail---and they do. Unexpected sources of help come from unpredictable quarters to people who are positive, enthusiastic and cheerful.

♦ ♦ ♦ ♦ ♦

Here are five rules for using your attitude to achieve success and happiness:

♦   Positive, healthy attitudes are not the results of success and happiness. Success and happiness are the results of positive attitudes.

♦   Your attitude toward others determines their attitude toward you.

♦   Before you can achieve the kind of life you want, you must think, act, talk and conduct yourself in all your affairs as would the person you wish to become.

♦   It is your attitude at the beginning of a task which more than anything else will influence its successful outcome.

♦   Treat everyone you meet as the most important person on earth. Why? Because:

    ♦   They are the most important people as far as they are concerned.

    ♦   This is the way human beings should treat one another.

    ♦   People want admiration, respect and self-esteem. They want the feeling that they are important, needed, respected. They will give their love, affection, respect, support and business to the person who fills that need.

Here are some simple suggestions for implementing these rules:

- Since your mind usually holds only one thought at a time, think positively and constructively.
- Radiate the attitude of well-being and confidence.
- Look for the best in people and ideas.
- Do not waste time talking about your problems or poor health.
- Know that your mind is limitless and that nothing is impossible. Accept that you have the freedom to choose the thoughts in your own mind.
- Always act as if you were the most successful person on earth. It will become a habit and you will be on your way to success and happiness.

Have you ever considered the idea that your life reflects the true picture of yourself? Similarly, attitude is the reflection of a person. The picture you project, the way you communicate to everyone you meet is a reflection of your total personality. The picture you project is determined by how you feel inside. What is going on inside shows up on the outside. If you do not like your world, change and become the kind of person you would really like to be. Your world will soon change to reflect the new you.

To generate a positive attitude, try being creative and flexible. Rigid people often find themselves stuck in life. They feel trapped by their circumstances. Attitude, being internal, can keep you cheerful, regardless of the environment in which circumstances may have placed you.

Changing thoughts changes realities. If you want to change attitudes, start with a change in behavior. Begin to act the part, as well as you can, of the person you want to become. The trick is in understanding that you must first become that which you seek. You can change. You can form new habits.

Create a mental image of the person you want to become. Then, begin now to act as that person would act in everything you do. Your life will not be transformed overnight. There will be no sudden miracle, but steadily, day by day, you will grow into the image you hold in your mind. Gradually, almost imperceptibly, you will become that person.

As you begin to act with more confidence, you will find that confidence is the first step to accomplishment. If you act a certain way long enough, you will eventually form the habit of being that kind of person. When things look bleak, remember that you have the power to change them. Whatever you are looking for---happiness, success, riches, peace or great accomplishments---must first be found within you.

Leo Buscaglia, a renowned college professor, gives a wonderful example of the right, positive attitude: "I'm always telling teachers it's impossible for children to deal with a concept that out of 50, they got 49 wrong. Why not tell them: 'Johnny, you got one right! Bravo!

Tomorrow we're going to make it two!'" See the difference between negative and positive thinking?

The happiest people are not the people without problems. They are the people who know how to solve their problems. You might be amazed at how easily you can solve your problems when you approach them with the right attitude. All problems become smaller if, instead of indulging them, you confront them. For example, touch a sharp thistle timidly, and it pricks you. Grasp it boldly, and its spine crumbles. If you take the attitude that things are not always going to be peaches and cream, you will be happy and thankful when they do go well, and you will avoid dismay when they do not go as you had hoped.

♦ ♦ ♦ ♦ ♦

Ultimately you control your own attitude. The right attitude gives you an uncanny control over your future. With conscious practice, it is astonishing how every aspect of your life can be changed for the better. Tell yourself you are great, terrific and excellent. Nothing great ever happens on the "okay" level. Make sure your dreams are the strongest influence on your daily decisions and activities. Then, you will face the future with eager anticipation, knowing you have planned an exciting future. Your future does not get better by hope. It gets better by plan, design and proper attitude.

SELECTED THOUGHTS ON ATTITUDE

There is very little difference in people, but that little difference makes a big difference. The little difference is attitude. The big difference is whether it is positive or negative. *CLEMENT STONE*

It is our attitude toward events, not the events themselves, which we can control. *EPICTETUS*

The ideal man bears the accidents of life with dignity and grace, making the best of the circumstances. *ARISTOTLE*

For success, attitude is equally as important as ability. *HARRY F. BANKS*

Attitude determines your altitude. *HARRY F. BANKS*

Things turn out best for the people who make the best of the way things turn out. *JOHN WOODEN*

The great thing about the human mind is that once it is programmed for a certain expectation, it will propel all action and behavior to fulfill that expectation. *DENIS WAITLEY*

Success or failure in business is caused more by mental attitude even than by mental capacities. *WALTER DILL SCOTT*

Man is not what he thinks he is; but what he thinks, he is. *ELBERT HUBBARD*

Success or failure depends solely on one's attitude.
All things are conquerable. It's simply a matter of
beliefs and accompanying attempts.
DAVID V. A. AMBROSE

Happiness is not a matter of good fortune or worldly
possessions. It's a mental attitude. It comes from
appreciating what we have, instead of being
miserable about what we do not have. It's so simple,
yet so hard for the human mind to comprehend.
JOHN LUTHER

We either build or destroy relationships by our
attitudes and expectations of ourselves and others.
JOE BATTEN

The world of achievement has always belonged to
the optimist. *J. HAROLD WILKINS*

Youth is not a time of life---it is a state of mind.
ANONYMOUS

The experiences of (concentration) camp life show
that man does have a choice of action. We who lived
in concentration camps can remember the men who
walked through the huts to comfort others, giving
away their last piece of bread. They may have been
few in number, but they offered sufficient proof that
everything can be taken from a man but one thing:
the last of the human freedoms--the freedom to
choose one's attitude in any given set of
circumstances, to choose one's own way.
VIKTOR FRANKL, "Man's Search for Meaning"

The longer I live, the more I realize the impact of attitude on life. Attitude to me, is more important than facts. It is more important than the past, than education, than money, than circumstances, than failures, than successes, than what other people think or say or do. It is more important than appearance, giftedness or skill. It will make or break a company...a church...a home...a marriage...a family. The remarkable thing is we have a choice every day regarding the attitude we will embrace for that day. We cannot change our past...we cannot change the fact that people will act in a certain way. We cannot change the inevitable. The only thing we can do is play on the one string we have, and that is our attitude...I am convinced that life is 10% what happens to me and 90% how I react to it. And so it is with you...we are in charge of our attitudes.
CHARLES SWINDOLL

Seek respect mainly from thyself, for it comes first from within. *STEVEN H. COOGLER*

The person with a healthy attitude toward his world recognizes his inferiorities as a normal part of being human. *EARL NIGHTINGALE*

TIME

There is time for everything. *THOMAS EDISON*

♦ ♦ ♦ ♦ ♦

I get very perturbed and unnecessarily frustrated when someone who has failed to do something gives the excuse: "I didn't have time." That is utter nonsense. When someone uses that excuse, what they are really saying is: "I didn't do it because that particular activity just wasn't high enough on my priority list."

We must understand and appreciate that we all have time to do the things we really want. We all do the really necessary things like sleeping, eating and going to the bathroom. After that, life is simply a matter of priorities.

All the time you will ever have is the present moment and the future. Today and tomorrow can be anything you want them to be, but it is amazing to discover what a small amount of time we actually spend earning a living and preparing for the future. The important thing about time is not to waste it on activities that do nothing to help you grow or that do not bring enjoyment. Never find yourself with time on your hands. Always be sure you are enjoying the time of your life.

Few people admit to having enough time, but we all have all the time there is. You never "get" time. You have to "make" time for the most important things. Think of time as an equal opportunity employer. You have exactly the same number of minutes and hours each day as everyone else. Successful people use each spare moment. The only way to "gain" time is to use it wisely. Winners use their time well. Losers waste their time.

Your personal effectiveness will be determined by your ability to manage your time well. There is always enough time to do the important things and there is never enough time to do everything. Identify your goals and make detailed plans for their accomplishment. Prioritize your activities. Focus on the vital few rather than the trivial many. Effective people do:

- First things first
- One thing at a time

Never let the fear of time stand in your way. The time will pass anyway, whether or not you are making good use of it. What overwhelms us is not the work or the task itself. It is thinking how hard and how time consuming it is going to be. It is seeing the task get bigger every day. It is putting it off and hoping that somehow, through some miracle, it will disappear. If there is something you have been wanting to do and you have been putting it off, begin it now! Then work hard at it---one day at a time!

Make a list of all the projects you have, or want to accomplish. Pick the one thing that is most important. Then, begin doing it. Do a little bit each day. And before you know it, the time will have passed and you will have completed your project. With it, you will have achieved a new competence, a new satisfaction and ultimate success in your efforts. There is an unbelievably positive cumulative effect of a little time well spent every day.

◆ ◆ ◆ ◆ ◆

Here are principles for proper time management:

◆ Commit to using your time wisely and effectively. Set aside time each day for thinking, reflecting and planning.

◆ Implement a "do it now" philosophy. Develop a sense of urgency for accomplishment.

◆ Think on paper. Write down your plans, ideas and responsibilities.

◆ Prioritize the items on your list in their order of importance.

  ◆ Work from that list.
  ◆ Concentrate on one thing at a time.
  ◆ Stick with that one thing until it is 100% complete.
  ◆ If it is not on the list, do not do it.

◆ Discipline yourself to get up each day and do your most important job first---even though you might not feel like it.

◆ Use the idea of "single handling." Handle papers only once until that job is finished.

◆ Use your "idle" time wisely. Practice simulation. Whatever you want to do, go over and over it in your mind until you have it letter perfect. It is a fun exercise and a great way to use time you would otherwise be wasting (in traffic, on telephone "hold," taking a shower). Then watch how well you perform when you actually face the situation.

Just one hour a day devoted to your special goal, e.g. study, an interesting or demanding project, or the refinement of a particular talent can make you an expert and provide you joy, success and happiness.

◆ ◆ ◆ ◆ ◆

Good time management becomes a first-rate habit made second nature. Some habits are time-savers. Others waste time. It takes willpower to replace our time-wasting habits with good habits.

William James, the great American psychologist, suggested four key ways to replace bad habits with good ones:

◆   Put your new habit into use immediately.
◆   Launch the new habit with strength and commitment.
◆   Practice the new habit without exception until it is firmly rooted.
◆   Don't give up!

A good place to begin is to keep an accurate, detailed time log for two weeks. Write down all your activities as they occur and how much time they take. You will identify your bad habits and your greatest time-wasting activities. Then you can adjust your activities to make better use of your time.

◆ ◆ ◆ ◆ ◆

Watching television is one of the greatest time-wasters. When you review your two week time log, you will probably be staggered when you see how much time you have wasted watching television. The average American spends an incredible 28 hours a week watching television. That is 16.6% of your life. If that person also sleeps eight hours a day, that is another 33.3%. So, the average American spends 50% of his life either asleep or in front of T.V. Seems like a very poor use of time, opportunity and life!

♦ ♦ ♦ ♦ ♦

You have the time and the opportunity to do or become anything you want. If you do not understand this very important fact, you are only kidding yourself.

SELECTED THOUGHTS ON TIME

Waste of time is the most extravagant of all expense.
THEOPHRASTUS

Dost thou love life? Then do not squander time, for that's the stuff life is made of.
BENJAMIN FRANKLIN

The busier we are, the more acutely we feel that we live. *IMMANUEL KANT*

We have only so much time to spend here---none of us knows how much. It's such a waste to spend any of it---any of it at all---in ways we do not find interesting or enjoyable. *EARL NIGHTINGALE*

We all find time to do what we really want to do.
WILLIAM FEATHER

You will never find time for anything. If you want
time, you must make it. *CHARLES BUXTON*

One of the illusions is that the present hour is not the
critical, decisive hour. Write it in your heart that
every day is the best day of the year.
RALPH WALDO EMERSON

This time, like all times, is a good one if we just
know what to do with it.
RALPH WALDO EMERSON

A man who dares to waste one hour of time has not
discovered the value of life. *CHARLES DARWIN*

Great things have no fear of time. *ANONYMOUS*

If a person gives you his time, he can give you no
more precious gift. *FRANK TYGER*

Be always resolute with the present hour. Every
moment is of infinite value. *GOETHE*

You can tell how a person has used his time
in the past by observing the manner in which
he lives today. *DENIS WAITLEY*

Perfection is attained by slow degrees; she requires
the hand of time. *VOLTAIRE*

A thought for each day: Make it through
until tomorrow. *ROBERT HALF*

Seek this very minute, whatever you can do, or dream you can; begin it. Boldness has genius, power and magic in it. Only engage and the mind grows heated; begin and then the task will be completed.
GOETHE

Employ thy time well if thou meanest to gain leisure.
BENJAMIN FRANKLIN

For truth and duty it is ever the fitting time; who waits until circumstances completely favor his undertaking, will never accomplish anything.
MARTIN LUTHER

Time will reveal everything. It is a babbler and speaks even when not asked. *EURIPIDES*

It's not the hours you put in that count; it's what you put into the hours. *EARL NIGHTINGALE*

Those who do the least always seem to have the least time. *ARNOLD GLASGOW*

Patience and time do more than strength or passion.
JEAN DE LA FONTAINE

Those who have most to do, and are willing to work, will find the most time. *SAMUEL SMILES*

Take time to enjoy the present.
ALEXANDER REID MARTIN

Know the true value of time; snatch, seize and enjoy
every moment of it. No idleness, no laziness, no
procrastination. *LORD CHESTERFIELD*

It doesn't pay to live in the past.
There's no future in it. *ANONYMOUS*

6

CRITICAL ELEMENTS FOR ACHIEVEMENT

DO YOUR OWN THING

If one advances confidently in the direction of his own dreams and endeavors to lead the life which he has imagined, he will meet with a success unimagined in common hours.
HENRY DAVID THOREAU

The preamble to the United States Constitution says "All men are created equal." Much as we would like to believe this adage, it is just not true. Some people are big, others small; some are smart, others not-so-smart; some pretty, others unattractive; some athletic, others musical, etc. With unequal innate abilities and assets, it is impossible to achieve equal results. We are not all created equal. But, we all enjoy equal opportunity to utilize our abilities! It is not what we have that is important. It is what we make of what we have.

There is a special place in this world for each of us. We should fit into our own place as comfortably as the last piece of a jigsaw puzzle. It is our unique niche. Our job is to find it. Anyone, regardless of age, gender or race, can find that interesting, exciting, challenging activity that inspires us and consumes us. It becomes our purpose in life, our reason for being.

It is never too late to find your niche and capitalize on it. (Colonel Sanders started Kentucky Fried Chicken at age 62!) The important thing is to make sure you take charge of your life and try to fit into your unique, warm, comfortable space where you can "do your own thing." We need to love what we are doing, living fully, enjoying each day and savoring the joy and excitement of life itself. We should live the life that we know deep down in our hearts is best for us.

♦ ♦ ♦ ♦ ♦

Unfortunately, many people spend the working week, Monday through Friday, five-sevenths of their lives, doing something they do not like, so that they can enjoy Saturday and Sunday, only two-sevenths of the week.

Spending five days a week, eight hours a day, doing something you hate is tragic. Enjoying only less than one-third of your life is no way to live. I know. I did that once. For six months, I worked in the advertising department of a small manufacturing company. I hated it. Work started at 8:30 a.m. I got there every day at 8:29 and immediately started watching the clock. I couldn't wait for 12:00 and lunch. I returned from lunch at 12:59 and started watching the clock again, eagerly awaiting 5:00. Time dragged. That clock just wouldn't move! It was awful---the worst work-related experience of my life.

Finally, I was either very smart, fortunate, totally frustrated, or all three! I decided to quit my job and take some time to "find myself." What was I going to do with the rest of my life? Certainly not spend it doing something I hated. My mother gave me the normal lecture you'd expect from a devoted, well-intentioned mother. "You should not quit. You've got a good job, with a good company and a good opportunity." That was true. The problem was, it was not right for me. I hated it and was determined not to spend the rest of my life doing something I hated.

Now, more than 25 years later, I am doing something I love, something I am absorbed in, something I think about constantly. My work is creative, challenging, and rewarding. When I go to sleep at night, I literally cannot wait to get up the next morning and get to work. A workaholic? I think not. I do work long and hard, but not at the expense of more important things (remember the priority list!): personal exercise and lots of time with my family. It is possible to achieve the proper balance between family, play and work.

♦ ♦ ♦ ♦ ♦

What do you enjoy doing? What would you like to do more than anything? If you really want to become happy, successful and probably rich (at least psychologically, if not financially) in the process, find work you enjoy so much you would do it for free. It is a strange paradox that if you can find something you would do for nothing and do it day after day, month in and month out, year in and year out (one day at a time!) you maximize your chances of becoming rich.

Ask yourself these questions:

♦ What would you do for free?
♦ What would you do if you were rich and did not need the money, but did have to work?
♦ What would you do with your life if you knew you were going to die in six months and had to work until then?

"Do your own thing"---what you enjoy, what is fun, what comes easily to you, what you are good at. Each of us is born to be a star at something. We have to discover that something and then spend time nurturing, developing, and perfecting it. Success and happiness is a matter of finding yourself and building upon what you find.

Take what you have and enjoy it. Make your life work on your terms, cultivating your own sense of purpose and your own sense of mission. Your brain is a unique asset. Use it and reach your own decisions. You can "do your own thing." You can establish your own self-worth because your self-worth is totally and absolutely determined by what you choose to think about yourself.

You have latent talent and ability that you never use simply because you are seldom called upon to really stretch. So do not be afraid to attempt the difficult, to reach beyond yourself for things and accomplishments unknown to the majority of people. That is the way you grow. If it is something you want to do very much, and you know it is right for you, try it. Stay with it. Chances are the power you need will be there at the right time. Get absorbed in what you are doing. You will surprise yourself with flashes of talent and brilliance you did not know you had.

♦ ♦ ♦ ♦ ♦

Mentally healthy people recognize and accept both their assets and their limitations. They have a reasonably accurate picture of themselves and they like what they see. Consider your strong points. Be yourself. "Do your own thing." If you spend your life trying to emulate others, you are doomed to a life of frustration and despair. You never become the best you can be by imitating others.

Imitation is suicide. Envy is ignorance. If you develop your own powers, you have no need for imitation or envy. You can be as happy and as successful as anyone, if you build on the powers within you. In all walks of life, the most successful people are the risk takers. Believe in your own ideas. Strike out on your own goals. Stand up for what you believe to be right. Take the risk of being different. When you find yourself, you will have a wonderful feeling that says, "This is it. I have found it. I am on the right road at last."

Remember, "we become what we think about." We become what we choose to become, whether or not we realize it. Get into the habit of forming your own independent opinions through study, research and, most importantly, personal observation. Do not worry about what other people think or say. If you believe what most people tell you, you will be wrong most of the time.

My philosophy is to look carefully at what "most people" are doing and then do exactly the opposite. Why? Because "most people" are negative, unhappy, unsuccessful, overweight, out-of-shape, poor, unimaginative, bored, uneducated, etc. So, is it not logical and rational to try to do, and be, exactly the opposite?

◆ ◆ ◆ ◆ ◆

Nietzsche said, "This is my way. What is your way? The way doesn't exist." What is your way? Do your own thing and never give up. The results will astound you!

◆ ◆ ◆ ◆ ◆

For many years, the words from two of my favorite songs have been particularly meaningful and relevant. These words have provided personal inspiration to "do my own thing," and to be my own person.

Frank Sinatra sang "My Way" (written by Paul Anka) and Sammy Davis, Jr. sang "I Gotta Be Me."

My Way

And now, the end is near and so I face the final curtain
My friends, I'll say it clear and state my case of which
I'm certain
I've lived a life that's full, I've traveled each and every
highway
And more, much more than this, I did it my way

Regrets, I've had a few, and then again too few to
mention
I did what I had to do, and saw it through without
exemption
I planned each charted course, each careful step along
the highway
And more, much more than this, I did it my way

What are we all? What have you really got?
If not yourself, then you have not
Just say the things you truly feel
And not the words of one who kneels
The record shows, I took the blows and did it my way

I Gotta Be Me

Whether I'm right or whether I'm wrong
Whether I find a place in this world or never belong,
I gotta be me, I gotta be me
What else can I be but what I am

I wanta live, not merely survive
And I won't give up this dream of life that keeps me
alive
I gotta be me, I gotta be me
The dream that I see makes me what I am

That faraway prize, a world of success
Is waiting for me if I heed the call
I won't settle down, won't settle for less
As long as there's a chance that I can have it all

I'll go it alone, that's how it must be
I can't be right for somebody else if I'm not right for
me
I gotta be free, I gotta be free
Daring to try to do it or die, I've gotta be me

SELECTED THOUGHTS ON
"DO YOUR OWN THING"

If a man does not keep pace with his companions, perhaps it is because he hears a different drummer. Let him step to the music which he hears, however measured or far away. *HENRY DAVID THOREAU*

Who so would be a man would be a nonconformist.
RALPH WALDO EMERSON

To be what we are, and to become what we are
capable of becoming, is the only end of life.
ROBERT LOUIS STEVENSON

To be nobody-but-yourself--in a world which is doing
its best, night and day, to make you like everybody
else--means to fight the hardest battle which any
human being can fight, and never stop fighting.
E. E. CUMMINGS

The only freedom which deserves the name is that of
pursuing our own good, in our own way, so long as
we do not attempt to deprive others of theirs, or
impede their efforts to obtain it.
JOHN STUART MILL

This above all, to thine own self be true, and it must
follow, as the night the day, thou canst not then be
false to any man. *WILLIAM SHAKESPEARE*

Let each of us become all that we are
capable of being. *THOMAS CARLYLE*

Men do less than they ought, unless they do all
that they can. *THOMAS CARLYLE*

Let every man practice the art that he knows best.
CICERO

What one does easily, one does well.
ANDREW CARNEGIE

No man is free who is not master of himself.
EPICTETUS

When looking back, usually I'm more sorry for
the things I didn't do than for the things I
shouldn't have done. *MALCOLM FORBES*

Making myself known is not what is uppermost
in my mind. I am aiming at something better; to
please myself. *GUSTAVE FLAUBERT*

The talent of success is nothing more than doing
what you can do well; and doing well whatever
you do, without a thought of fame.
HENRY WADSWORTH LONGFELLOW

I am I and you are you. I'm not in this world to live
up to your expectations and you're not in this world
to live up to mine. If we meet, it's beautiful. If not, it
can't be helped. *FRITZ PERLS*

When we cannot find contentment in ourselves, it is
useless to seek it elsewhere.
LA ROUCHEFOUCAULD

The most important thing is to love your sport. Never
do it to please someone else---it has to be yours. That
is all that will justify the hard work needed to
achieve success. Compete against yourself, not
others, for that is who is truly your best competition.
NORMAN VINCENT PEALE

The greatest thing in the world is to know how to
belong to oneself. *MICHEL DE MONTAIGNE*

We forfeit three-fourths of ourselves in order to be
like other people. *ARTHUR SCHOPENHAUER*

Crazy, he is! And that's fine, because being crazy gives me a wonderful latitude for behavior.
LEO BUSCAGLIA

To find out what one is fitted to do and to secure an opportunity to do it is the key to happiness.
JOHN DEWEY

Don't pretend to care and love when the truth is you're indifferent. Don't spend a lot of unnecessary time with people you don't like. Have the courage to know what you feel, and to live honestly, in accordance with what you feel, and with integrity.
NATHANIEL BRANDEN

Each of us has some wonderful ability, or talent, that is uniquely our own. This is what we should sell; this is what we should stay with. If the next pasture looks greener, it may be because it's getting better care.
EARL NIGHTINGALE

No one can live my life for me. If I am wise, I shall begin today to build my own truer and better world from within. *HORATIO W. DRESSER*

The most important person any player should work to be as good as is himself. Your own excellence, success and greatest pride comes from only one person--you. Your first responsibility is to be the best you can. There's nobody else like you, so why try to be like somebody else? *FRANK ROBINSON*

I'm a firm believer in the theory that people only do their best at things they truly enjoy. It is difficult to excel at something you don't enjoy.
JACK NICKLAUS

Make sure that the career you choose is one you enjoy. If you do not enjoy what you are doing, it will be difficult to give the extra time, effort and devotion it takes to be a success. If it is a career that you find fun and enjoyable, then you will do whatever it takes. You will give freely of your time and effort and you will not feel that you are making sacrifices in order to be a success. *KATHY WHITWORTH*

Your success depends upon you.
You have to steer your own course.
You have to do your own thinking.
You must make your own decisions.
You have to solve your own problems.
Your character is your handiwork.
You have to write your own record.
You have to build your own monument---or dig your own pit. Which are you doing?
B.C. FORBES

I cannot give you a formula for success, but I can give you the formula for failure--which is: Try to please everybody. *HERBERT BAYARD SWOPE*

We learned that the possibility for choosing a life that will give us the best we can dream of is there. It's ours for the asking. It's ours for the taking. It's ours to go after. *KEN DYCHTWALD*

After a while you learn the subtle difference between holding a hand and chaining a soul; And you learn that love doesn't mean leaning and company doesn't mean security; And you begin to learn that kisses aren't contracts and presents aren't promises; And you begin to accept your defeats with your head up and your eyes open, with the grace of an adult, not the grief of a child; And you learn to build all your roads on today because tomorrow's ground is too uncertain for plans. After a while you learn that even sunshine burns if you get too much. So plant your own garden and decorate your own soul, instead of waiting for someone to bring you flowers. And you learn that you really can endure...that you really are strong; and you really do have worth. *ANONYMOUS*

The mold of a man's fortune is in his own hands.
FRANCIS BACON

Let me have my own way exactly in everything, and a sunnier and pleasanter creature does not exist.
THOMAS CARLYLE

No one is any better than you, but you are no better than anyone else until you do something to prove it.
DONALD LAIRD

The most valuable thing I have learned from life is to regret nothing. *SOMERSET MAUGHAM*

To find a career to which you are adapted by nature and then to work hard at it, is about as near to a formula for success and happiness as the world provides. *MARK SULLIVAN*

A man has to live with himself and he should see to it that he always has good company.
CHARLES EVANS HUGHES

You have to develop a style that suits you and pursue it, not just develop a bag of tricks. Always be yourself. *JIMMY STEWART*

If we would understand others, we must first understand ourselves. *WILLIAM FEATHER*

Be civil to all; sociable to many; familiar with few.
BENJAMIN FRANKLIN

If you live what you believe, you will always have the respect of others. *DALE MURPHY*

Every human being is responsible for himself and not under obligation to meet the expectations of others.
FRITZ PERLS

You've got to learn to cultivate your own garden.
CANDIDE

DO YOUR BEST

You don't have to be the best. You should do your best. *PAUL HAMMER*

Good advice. After all, what is "the best?" Who is "the best?" Who is the best football quarterback, the best hitter or pitcher in baseball, the best author, the best teacher, the best whatever? How do you define "the best?" How do you decide "the best?" It makes for interesting, fun, heated discussions, with no definitive answers. So if your goal is to become "the best," you are probably setting yourself up for a disappointment. How can you assure yourself that you are, in fact, "the best?"

♦ ♦ ♦ ♦ ♦

My neighbor, returned from a business meeting where he heard Wally 'Famous Amos' the internationally known speaker. He was excited, motivated and enthused by Wally's philosophy:

♦   It is no good to say "I'll try."
♦   You must say "I will."
♦   Commitment is the answer.

On the plane home, he sat next to a man who had heard the same talk. The other man thought Wally was awful and had walked out in the middle of the talk. So, no matter who you are, how good you are and how happy you are with yourself, you cannot please everyone.

♦ ♦ ♦ ♦ ♦

All you can do is "do your best." If you commit to do your best, you can assure yourself ultimate success. As William James said, "If you will do each day as best you can the work which is before you, you will wake up one day and find yourself one of the competent ones of your generation."

SELECTED THOUGHTS ON "DO YOUR BEST"

There is no fun equal to the satisfaction of doing
one's best. *B.C. FORBES*

The secret to success is doing the best that you can
do. Forget about whether you might win or lose. By
working hard and practicing the skills that you need
to perform, the results will take care of themselves.
Being successful is doing your best.
BARBARA ANN COCHRAN

When we have done our best, we should await the
results in peace. *ANONYMOUS*

If you do the best you can, you will find nine times
out of ten, you have done as well or better than
anyone else. *WILLIAM FEATHER*

There is no substitute for hard work. There will be
disappointments but the "the harder you work, the
luckier you will get." Never be satisfied with less
than your very best effort. If you strive for the top
and miss, you'll still "beat the pack."
GERALD R. FORD

Be true to the best you know. This is your high ideal.
If you do your best, you cannot do more. Do your
best every day and your life will gradually expand
into satisfying fullness. *H. W. DRESSER*

You set a goal to be the best and then you work
every waking hour of each day trying to achieve
that goal. *DON SHULA*

The dictionary is the only place success comes before work. Hard work is the price we must all pay for success. I think we can accomplish almost anything if we are willing to pay the price. The price of success is hard work, dedication to the job at hand, and the determination that whether we win or lose, we have applied the best of ourselves to the task at hand.
VINCE LOMBARDI

I just believe that whatever it is you do, you should do the best you can. Put your all into it. If you don't utilize your talents, don't cultivate them, make them grow, then that's a shame. It's a sin, really.
HARRY CARSON

I never wanted to set records. The only thing I strived for was perfection. *WILT CHAMBERLAIN*

GOALS

What the mind of man can conceive and believe, it can achieve. *WILLIAM JAMES*

Life is what we decide it is going to be. We can do whatever we want. We are in charge. We have control. For most people, that thought is the problem. They never decide exactly what they want.

People do not have much trouble achieving goals. They can do that. The problem is they do not set goals in the first place. People do not plan to fail. They just fail to plan. They leave their success to chance, but chance does not work.

♦ ♦ ♦ ♦ ♦

Thomas Edison said genius is 1% inspiration and 99% perspiration. Most "geniuses" have ordinary intelligence and become geniuses because they use their minds and work harder than others do.

What are the qualities these geniuses enjoy?

♦   They have a creative, open mind that is receptive to new ideas and different ways of solving problems.

♦   They approach problems systematically using logical, orderly processes to reach sound, well thought out conclusions.

♦   They concentrate intensely and single-mindedly without diversion or distraction on one thing at a time. They concentrate all their mental powers on one single issue.

♦   They set goals. Nothing great was ever attained without concentrated effort and energy focused on a single objective. Successful people adopt a specific purpose that becomes all-consuming.

♦ ♦ ♦ ♦ ♦

Goals are destinations that have to be reached. They are more important than the time and effort that is required to achieve them. They are dreams seen in the mind and felt in the heart that are too big to be denied.

Goals require commitment. The biggest obstacle between us and our goals is a lack of total commitment. Until we become committed, we can allow ourselves to draw back. Without commitment, we are ineffective. Goals give us direction and purpose and help make us effective.

By establishing a goal, you focus your thinking and begin moving toward your goal. Carlisle wrote: "The man without a purpose, is like a ship without a rudder. Have a purpose in life, and having it, throw such strength of mind and muscle into it as God has given you. A man with a half volition goes backwards and forwards and makes no way on the smoothest road. A man with a whole volition advances on the roughest road and will reach his purpose if there be even a little wisdom in it."

Sailing successfully through life is simply a matter of progressively setting and achieving goals, one after the other, each a little better, more challenging than the former. Just like a ship, set out for one port of call at a time. Have faith in yourself---a quiet firm inner knowledge that you can and will accomplish your goals. The answers you seek will come to you in time if you keep looking for them and don't give up!

♦ ♦ ♦ ♦ ♦

Setting goals is the basis of success. Unless you can say in one concise sentence exactly what your goal is, the chances are good that you have not clearly defined it. You need to set specific goals. Why?

♦ Without goals, you will never fulfill your potential. Goals allow you to focus your thoughts, your time and your efforts. Your discontent is the distance between what you have and what you want. Setting goals is the first step toward reducing that distance.

♦ Success is simply setting and achieving goals. It is not easy and requires delaying gratification. The tendency in life is to do what is fun and easy rather than what is hard and necessary. The world seems to make room for people whose words and actions show that they know where they are going.

♦ Your goals must be consistent with your basic values. They have to be consistent with what you believe to be good, valuable and important.

♦ You must have a major definite purpose, one goal that is more important than any other. If you do not have a major definite purpose, make establishing one your first goal.

♦ Your goals must be in writing. They should be clear, specific and vivid. Writing them down programs them into your subconscious mind. If you do not write them down, either you do not know what they are or you are not committed to them. Rewrite your major goal every morning. This process reinforces your goal in your mind. Just like reading a road map before you start a trip, you know exactly where you are going and how to get there. You now have a clear commitment to future success.

Here are two examples of proper goal setting:

PERSONAL GOALS   ECONOMIC GOALS

♦ Stop smoking   ♦ Vacation
♦ Improve physical fitness   ♦ Furniture
♦ Lose weight   ♦ Car
♦ Be more decisive   ♦ Boat
♦ Be a better communicator   ♦ Home

Systematically, one day at a time, work on the first goal in each column. Do not think or worry about the others. Concentrate exclusively on your number one goal. Do whatever is necessary to accomplish goal number one.

The goal setting process should be fun, like a game. The fun part of having a list is being able to check off something when it is completed. Goal setting is not something you do just once. It is a continual, daily process. Your goals should be big, challenging, rewarding. They will allow you to grow to your full potential.

Goals are important but they must be flexible and adjustable. Remember, life should be fun. Goals are a means, not an end. Easy does it. All you need to do is decide exactly what you are trying to accomplish and set about it in a calm and deliberate manner. Calmness and serenity are important. Keep things in perspective. Trust your intuition. Make only those decisions that need to be made now. Arrange your time so you maximize the time spent working on your goals.

If you are honest with yourself about the things you want, you will find they can all be yours in a surprisingly short time---if you take things in order, one at a time. When you know what you want and you want it badly enough, the answers will come to you.

The way to really enjoy life best is to accomplish one goal and then start immediately on the next one. One success leads to another. There is a tremendous cumulative effect. There is an incredible force that seems to come to those who develop a healthy attitude and have established realistic goals. Sometimes we call it "getting lucky." That is not
 what it really is. It is a momentum that will give you all sorts of help once you are on your own way to success.

Become goal oriented. Goal oriented people make up their minds about exactly what they want and they keep their eyes and their enthusiasm on that goal until it becomes a reality in their lives. Decide on your goals. Insist on them. Do this every day and it will become a habit that will lead you continuously from one success to another.

SELECTED THOUGHTS ON GOALS

The most practical of all methods of controlling the mind is the habit of keeping it busy with a definite purpose, backed by a definite plan.
NAPOLEON HILL

Definiteness of purpose is the starting point of all achievement. *CLEMENT STONE*

Beware of what you set your heart upon. For it surely shall be yours. *RALPH WALDO EMERSON*

You must have long-range goals to keep you from being frustrated by short-range failures.
CHARLES C. NOBLE

When you determine what you want, you have made the most important decision of your life. You have to know what you want in order to attain it.
DOUGLAS LURTAN

When a man is in earnest, and knows what he is about, his work is half done.
COMTE DE MIRABEAU

Obstacles are those frightful things you see when you take your eyes off the goal. *HANNAH MORE*

If you don't know where you are going, every road will get you nowhere. *HENRY KISSINGER*

When you're goal-oriented, the hours of the day don't matter. All you regret is that there aren't enough of them. You eat, drink and sleep it, because you love it and you want it so much. *MALCOLM FORBES*

The way you enjoy life best is to wrap up one goal and start right on the next one. Don't linger too long at the table of success. The only way to enjoy another meal is to get hungry. *JIM ROHN*

Adhere to a definite, clear-cut purpose in life and push forward painstakingly, perseveringly and conscientiously to its realization. *B.C. FORBES*

Devote earnest effort to planning your life, to setting for yourself a goal. Winds and storms may--doubtless will--force you occasionally off your course, but surely it is better to have a course to follow than to float about rudderless and goalless. *B.C. FORBES*

Destiny is not a matter of chance, it is a matter of choice; it is not a thing to be waited for, it is a thing to be achieved. *WILLIAM JENNINGS BRYAN*

We need to know where we are going and how we plan to get there. Our dreams and aspirations must be translated into real and tangible goals with priorities and a time frame. All of this should be in writing, so that it can be reviewed, updated, and revised as necessary. *MERLIN OLSEN*

Take time to think and to pinpoint what's really important in your life. *ALEXANDER REID MARTIN*

Set goals in life; set them high and persist until they are achieved. Once they are achieved, set bigger and better goals. You will soon find that your life will become happier and more purposeful by working toward positive goals. *RAYMOND FLOYD*

Without organization and leadership toward a realistic goal, there is no chance of realizing more than a small percentage of your potential. *JOHN WOODEN*

Without a plan for completion, it just won't happen. *ROBERT HALF*

The man with average mentality, but with control, with a definite goal, and a clear conception of how it can be gained, and above all, with the power of application and labor, wins in the end. *WILLIAM HOWARD TAFT*

If you want to be an entrepreneur, you must be a dreamer. Dreams are what goals are made of. They are the motivating factor for hard work. Without them, you have nothing. *DENISE FUGO*

No life grows great until it is focused, dedicated, disciplined. *HARRY EMERSON FOSDICK*

One of the greatest obstacles to success is man's inability to put first things first. *CHARLES B. ROTH*

Keep a definite goal of achievement constantly in view. Realize that work well and worthily done makes life truly worth living. *GRENVILLE KLEISER*

LAWS

In your search for success and happiness, do not look for miracles, secrets or short cuts. You will not find any. Why? Because they do not exist.

What you will find are the eternal laws of nature. They have always been there and always will be. They are as rigid and certain and absolute as:

- ♦ The sun rising in the East.
- ♦ Night following day.
- ♦ Spring following winter.
- ♦ Gravity.

Here are some laws that have worked for me:

- ♦ Law of self-determination: You are now and you will become what you think about.
- ♦ Law of compensation: As ye sow, so shall ye reap.
- ♦ Law of accumulation: Life is cumulative! No honest effort is ever lost. Instead, every effort, small or large, accumulates and grows like a snowball rolling down a hill.
- ♦ Law of correspondence: As within, so without. Your outer life will always be a reflection of your inner self.
- ♦ Law of human conduct: Always make the other person feel important.
- ♦ Law of cultivation: Let each person become all that he was created capable of being.
- ♦ Mythical law of nature: The four things we crave most in life--happiness, success,

freedom and peace of mind--are always attained by giving them to someone else.

To achieve success and happiness you need only:

♦ Learn these absolute truths.
♦ Understand that they are unyielding and unfailing.
♦ Commit to following them.
♦ Reward yourself from time to time.
♦ Enjoy and take pride in your success.

SELECTED THOUGHTS ON LAWS

If one advances confidently in the direction of his dreams and endeavors to live the life which he has imagined, he will meet with a success unexpected in common hours. *HENRY DAVID THOREAU*

The journey of a thousand miles begins with a single step. *LAO TSE*

Act so that your principle of action might safely be a saw for the whole world. *IMMANUEL KANT*

7

TOPICS FOR PERSONAL WELL-BEING

LOVE

"Everybody's searching for a hero.
People need someone to look up to.
I never found anyone who fulfilled my needs.
A lonely place to be, and so I learned to depend on me.

I decided long ago, never to walk in anyone's shadow.
If I fail, if I succeed, at least I lived as I believe.
No matter what they take from me, they can't take
away my dignity.

Because the greatest love of all is happening to me.
I found the greatest love of all inside of me.

The greatest love of all is easy to achieve.
Learning to love yourself, it is the greatest love of all."

"The Greatest Love of All"
Sung by *Whitney Houston*

These words express my sentiments exactly. Treat everyone, especially yourself, with kindness, love, courtesy and respect. You come first. You should be your own first love affair. If you cannot or do not love yourself, you will not be able to love others.

♦ ♦ ♦ ♦ ♦

Here is a philosophy we should embrace if we choose to or decide to love someone: "I accept you and I love you, even when I do not understand you. You do not <u>earn</u> my love; you simply have it---unconditionally. You will always have my love and acceptance---regardless."

You do not have to spend time with anyone you do not want to, but you should accept others for who and what they are. You do not have the right to change others, just as they do not have the right to change you. You must either accept the person as he or she is or look for someone else with whom you are willing to share your time and space. Do not be too demanding or look for perfection. None of us is perfect.

Wayne Dyer has great words for love. He says love is forgiving. Forgiving is one word and it is also two words:

- ♦   One word - forgiving i.e. excuse, pardon.
- ♦   Two words - for giving - yours to give away, share with others and expect nothing back in return.

Great concept, isn't it?

♦　♦　♦　♦　♦

More and more you see relationships that are
deteriorating or have completely fallen apart.
Frequently, people cling to the past and try to hold on
to what "shoulda, woulda, coulda" been. Here is what
the "love" philosopher, Leo Buscaglia says:

> "The most difficult thing is to let go, and that is
> the truth. If somebody wants to leave you, and you
> hold on madly, and they have already gone
> spiritually--all they have left you is an empty
> body--that is an insult to you. Isn't it better to say,
> 'I want to be with you as long as we can grow
> together. And if you feel that I'm interfering with
> your growth, then maybe it is better for a while for
> you to go elsewhere.' What are you holding on
> to?"

SELECTED THOUGHTS ON LOVE

Perhaps love is the process of my leading you gently
back to yourself. *ANTOINE DE SAINT-EXUPERY*

Love is the act of extending oneself to nurture
another. *JANE LOHR*

Love is the single most powerful and potent force for
influencing and changing behaviors. *P. A. SOROKIN*

We are most of us very lonely in this world; you who have any who love you, cling to them and thank God. *WILLIAM MAKEPEACE THACKERAY*

The truly important things in life--love, beauty and one's own uniqueness--are constantly being overlooked. *PABLO CASALS*

Have the courage to love. Since love costs nothing to give or to take, you've got nothing to lose. *LEO BUSCAGLIA*

I think growing into a loving person is a little like becoming an artist. You start with yourself, then you learn by imitating the "masters"---parents, writers, film makers---and finally, with everyone else's experiences rattling around in your head, you begin to absorb it all and find your own form. *LENA TABORI*

Love at first sight is easy to understand. It's when two people have been looking at each other for years that it becomes a miracle. *SAM LEVINSON*

The trouble with some women is that they get all excited about nothing - and then marry him. *CHER*

KINDNESS

Be kind, for everyone you meet is
fighting a hard battle. *PHILO*

Be nice, pleasant, courteous, and loving to all you
meet. Simply smile and give them a warm hello.

It is just as easy to be happy, warm, and kind to people
as it is to be curt, nasty and mean. It takes no more
time or effort. The results are amazing because your
positive behavior makes you feel even better than the
small joys you bring to others. Try it for just one day.
Treat everyone you come in contact with as the most
important person on earth. To them, they are.

Thirty years ago, I bought furniture from a wonderful
man, John Sedlak. Every time you asked him, "How
are you, John?", he responded: "Fantastic!" That
enthusiastic, positive response impressed me. I thought
I would try it, too. So when people ask me: "How are
you?", I always answer: "Terrific!" Now, people with
whom I speak automatically expect me to answer,
"Terrific." They don't even bother to ask: "How are
you?" They just say, "I know--you are terrific." One
person even has nick-named me, "Tom Terrific."

This "terrific" attitude does two things. It really makes
me think, walk, talk and act "terrific." And other
people think I am "terrific" because, in a positive, non-
bragging manner, I keep telling them so. It is an
automatic conversation opener for everyone to say,

"How are you?" So twenty, thirty or forty times a day I am telling myself and everyone I meet that I am terrific. I am now convinced that I am terrific.

♦ ♦ ♦ ♦ ♦

My two children are wonderful and special. (What would you expect me to say about my kids?) I get frequent compliments from their teachers, friends and their friends' parents. I always respond: "Thank you very much. That is nice to hear. I appreciate the compliment. What makes you say that?" The response is usually: "Jenny/Adam is always so nice and polite. Whenever she/he sees me, she/he smiles and says: 'Hello, Mrs. Wiggins.' Their sweetness, politeness and attention make me feel good."

Isn't that amazing!? Their simple, kind act of:

♦   Smiling
♦   Saying hello
♦   Using the person's name has put them on pedestals. They feel good about themselves and have made others feel good about themselves too.

How difficult, how time consuming is it to say three words: "Hello, Mrs. Wiggins." You do not have to be a genius or even smart---just kind and thoughtful. Can't we all make our lives happier, more pleasant, by smiling and saying hello to everyone we see?

♦ ♦ ♦ ♦ ♦

Kindness comes easiest when we give it away. When you have kind, positive thoughts in your mind and heart, your words and actions reflect this kindness. You achieve calmness, tranquility and a deep inner peace.

SELECTED THOUGHTS ON KINDNESS

Resolve to be tender with the young, compassionate with the aging, sympathetic with the striving and tolerant of the weak because sometime in your life, you will have been all of these.
GEORGE WASHINGTON CARVER

Kindness always pays, but it pays best when not done for pay. *ANONYMOUS*

Kindness is a form of riches on which you don't have to pay tax. *ROADSIDE BILLBOARD*

The best portion of a good man's life is his little, nameless, unremembered acts of kindness and love.
WILLIAM WORDSWORTH

The best happiness insurance is kindness. The premiums are thoughtfulness. *ARNOLD GLASGOW*

The biggest things in life are the small kindnesses.
FRANK TYGER

LIFE

When it's time to die, let us not discover that we have never lived. *HENRY DAVID THOREAU*

There is a huge difference between living a full, wonderful, exciting, positive, productive life and barely existing or surviving. How and why we live is much more important than simply living.

Your life should be an exciting adventure. It should never be boring. Live fully. Be alive. Be eager and delighted to get out of bed every day. Each day should be the most interesting, wonderful day of your life. If your life doesn't hold abundant joy, it is not because of your restricted circumstances. It is because you are not utilizing the rules we have established.

Life is too short to waste doing anything you do not really enjoy. You are born and exist to be successful and outstanding at something. You have to discover your unique talents and then spend years developing them. Live the life that you know deep down in your heart you would like to live. You should be doing work you like to do because you do it exceptionally well.

The purpose of life is to enjoy it. The joy in life is the daily journey, not the final destination. Life's road is a series of turning points. They never end. They make life mysterious and fascinating. Take each turn as it appears, enjoying the present day because it is the only one you will ever have. Make each day complete, whole, fulfilling and exciting. Be sure you are having the time of your life.

◆ ◆ ◆ ◆ ◆

Here are six thoughts I developed that hopefully put life in its proper perspective:

- ◆ Calm down
- ◆ Take care of one thing at a time
- ◆ Everything is going to be O.K.
- ◆ No one said "when"
- ◆ It doesn't matter anyway
- ◆ In the long run, we're all dead

SELECTED THOUGHTS ON LIFE

The most valuable thing I have learned from life is to regret nothing. *SOMERSET MAUGHAM*

Business and life are like a bank account--you can't take out more than you put in. *WILLIAM FEATHER*

Fear not that thy life shall come to an end, but rather fear that it shall never have a beginning.
JOHN CARDINAL NEWMAN

Life is what happens to us while we are making other plans. *THOMAS LA MANCE*

One never finds life worth living. One always has to make it worth living. *HARRY EMERSON FOSDICK*

All is for the best in the best of all possible worlds.
VOLTAIRE

He who has a why to live for can bear
almost any how. *VICTOR FRANKL*

My life seems like one long obstacle course, with me
as the chief obstacle. *JACK PAAR*

A great life, a great home and family, a great career,
a great business, a great accomplishment of any
kind--all these come with patience--patience with
others, with the world and with ourselves.
EARL NIGHTINGALE

Life is not a problem to be solved, but a reality to be
experienced. *SOREN KIERKEGAARD*

The quality of life is more important than life itself.
ALEXIS CARREL

The important thing in life is to have a great aim
and to possess the aptitude and the perseverance
to attain it. *GOETHE*

Life is like an ice cream cone, you have to
learn to lick it. *CHARLES M. SCHULZ*

We must have courage to bet on our ideas, to
take the calculated risk, and to act. Everyday
living requires courage if life is to be effective
and bring happiness. *MAXWELL MALTZ*

Live not one's life as though one had a thousand
years, but live each day as the last.
MARCUS AURELIUS

128

To get the best and most out of life, put the best and most of yourself into it. *B.C. FORBES*

Life is tons of discipline. *ROBERT FROST*

The only thing constant in life is change. *LA ROUCHEFOUCAULD*

While we are postponing, life speeds by. *SENECA*

If you would only recognize that life is hard, things would be so much easier for you. *LOUIS BRANDEIS*

So live--decently, fearlessly, joyously--don't forget that in the long run it is not the years in your life but the life in your years that counts! *ADLAI E. STEVENSON*

Look to this day, for it is life, the very life of life. In this day's brief pause lies all the verities and realities of your existence. The bliss of growth. The glory of action. The splendor of beauty. For yesterday is gone and tomorrow is only a vision. But today well lived makes of every yesterday a dream of happiness, and every tomorrow a dream of hope. *ANCIENT PRAYER*

The quality of a person's life is in direct proportion to their commitment to excellence regardless of their chosen field of endeavor. *VINCENT T. LOMBARDI*

While alive, live. *MALCOLM FORBES*

There is no wealth but life. *JOHN RUSKIN*

Believe that life is worth living and your belief will
help create the fact. *WILLIAM JAMES*

You've got a life to live. It's short, at best.
It's a wonderful privilege and a terrific
opportunity---and you've even been equipped
for it. Use your equipment, give it all you've got.
Love your neighbor---he's having just as much
trouble as you are. Be nice to him; be kind to him.
Trust God and work hard.
NORMAN VINCENT PEALE

All animals except man know that the principal
business of life is to enjoy it. *SAMUEL BUTLER*

How do you know when you're old? When you
double your current age and realize you're not going
to live that long. *MICHAEL J. LEYDEN II*

City Life: millions of people being lonesome
together. *HENRY DAVID THOREAU*

There are two things to aim at in life: first to get
what you want; and after that to enjoy it. Only the
wisest of people achieve the second.
LOGAN PERSALL SMITH

FEELINGS

No one can make you feel inferior without
your consent. *ELEANOR ROOSEVELT*

Two of our major goals should be to:

- Feel good about ourselves.
- Be the person we want to be.

When you have that overwhelmed feeling, that pit of
the stomach ache, that mild panic that you are losing
control, try this seven-step philosophy:

- Slow down.
- Relax.
- Regain control.
- Be yourself.
- Consider your strong points.
- Do what you can effectively today.
- Leave the rest until tomorrow.

When you are down, depressed, upset, sad, unhappy,
overwhelmed, discouraged or frustrated, think
positively. Follow the wisdom of Wayne Dyer:

> "This is what has happened, and I'm not going to
> choose these reactions. I'm not going to choose to
> be immobilized and depressed. I'm not going to
> pretend I like it. I'm just not going to allow myself
> to be immobilized by it. I won't. I will get through
> the next five minutes. I will get through the next
> five minutes, and that is how I will handle it."

♦ ♦ ♦ ♦ ♦

One thing that is most destructive to feeling good about yourself is guilt. You may feel that others (your parents, your spouse, your boss, your significant other) make you feel guilty. Wrong! No one else makes you feel guilty. You do it to yourself.

There are four ways to handle guilt:

- ♦ Realize that only you can make yourself feel guilty.
- ♦ Choose to stop whatever behavior you are feeling guilty about.
- ♦ Stop telling yourself that you are a bad person because of the particular behavior you are feeling guilty about.
- ♦ Forgive everybody, including yourself, for what has happened. Rid yourself of the negative emotions that make you feel guilty.

♦ ♦ ♦ ♦ ♦

As I have stressed over and over, you can control your thoughts. Since your feelings come directly from your thoughts, you can therefore control your feelings. You can control your feelings by learning to control the way you think.

THINK AND THEN, "JUST DO IT"

A man is what he thinks about all day long.
RALPH WALDO EMERSON

We have learned that:

♦ Man's unique gift is his ability to reason. Only human beings use logic and reason.
♦ We become what we think about.
♦ We can control our thoughts. What we think is up to us.
♦ We are the sum total of our thoughts.
♦ We are completely responsible for our own success in life.
♦ We are where we are because that is exactly where we want to be.
♦ There is a fine line between what we expect from life and what we get. If we are not getting what we like, it is because our expectations are too low.

With this powerful road map to success and happiness, why do people fail? When asked this question, the great humanitarian and educator Dr. Albert Sweitzer responded: "Men simply don't think." A shame isn't it?

Why don't people think? Probably because we take our mind for granted. Since it came to us as standard equipment and was free, we do not value it enough. As crazy as it sounds, the things we have to pay for (houses, cars, jewelry, etc.) are the things we value. Exactly the opposite should be true.

Everything really worthwhile in life comes to us free: our minds, hearts, bodies, souls, intelligence, dreams, ambitions and aspirations. We need to appreciate our irreplaceable and priceless assets and utilize them every day. Just a few minutes each day of deliberate thinking works wonders for our mind, for our outlook on life and for our future happiness and success. Be certain to make time each day to reflect, to think and to plan.

♦ ♦ ♦ ♦ ♦

But, simply reflecting, thinking, dreaming and planning are not enough. You can reflect, think, dream and plan all you want, but you also must <u>DO</u>! Knowledge isn't power. Applied knowledge is power. Action is the key. Think action.

Eliminate from your thinking and your vocabulary such words as "can't" and "impossible." You must realize that at some point you must perform. You must convert those dreams into realities. As a youth, I was fortunate that my mother taught me a wise adage: "Actions speak louder than words." You can talk all you want but, eventually, you must do. The doers are the happy and successful people in this world.

I have worked long and hard to try to convince my children that the word "can't" doesn't exist. Anything is possible. It is simply a matter of:

♦   Deciding what you want.
♦   Figuring out a way to accomplish it.
♦   Finding the person who can say "yes."

Adam is an avid tennis player. Early in the seventh grade, he complained that weight lifting in gym class was hurting his shoulder and affecting his tennis workouts. I asked Adam: "Why don't we get you out of gym?" He said: "You <u>can't</u> do that. Everyone has to take gym." I said: "You have forgotten, <u>can't</u> doesn't exist. By the way, what time do you have gym?" He said: "First period." I said: "Why don't we get you out of gym and before school in the mornings you can go to the Racquet Club and practice your tennis?" He said: "You <u>can't</u> do that. They won't allow it." I immediately accepted this opportunity. I was challenged to prove conclusively to him that "<u>can't</u> doesn't exist."

To make a long story short, by nine o'clock the following morning, I had met with Adam's school principal and explained the situation. He agreed:

- ♦ That the current situation was not in this student's best interest.
- ♦ A course of "independent study" could be established that would allow Adam to devote his normal physical education time and effort directly to tennis.

You should have seen the smile on Adam's face when I told him how the situation had been resolved, exactly as I had suggested it would be. With a big smile on my face, I reiterated the fact that "<u>can't</u>" doesn't exist!

♦ ♦ ♦ ♦ ♦

Interestingly, one day several months later, Adam came home from school quite distressed. The daily school schedule had been altered so that first period (his normal tennis time) was held last period. Adam dutifully attended his regular gym class. The gym teacher asked Adam who he was and why he hadn't been to gym for the last several months? When Adam explained that he was pursuing "independent study," the gym teacher said: "That's impossible! We don't have independent study here." Adam was understandably rattled and asked me what to do. I told him: "Don't worry about it. Your independent study program was established by the person who could say 'yes,' not the gym instructor who could only say 'no.'"

The next morning, after another short visit with the principal, the matter was promptly resolved to everyone's (Adam's, my and the principal's) satisfaction.

To repeat emphatically: <u>Can't doesn't exist</u>! Anything is possible. It is simply a matter of:

- ♦   Deciding what you want.
- ♦   Figuring out a way to accomplish it.
- ♦   Finding the person who can say "yes."

It's no secret that there are many talkers and few doers. Which are you? More importantly, which will you be tomorrow and for the rest of your life?

SELECTED THOUGHTS ON
THINK AND "JUST DO IT"

There is nothing either good or bad, but
thinking makes it so. *SHAKESPEARE*

No man ever got very far--and stayed there--who did
not spend a vast amount of brain-sweat, who did not
think things out for himself, who did not try to map
out his own course, to steer his own ship.
B.C. FORBES

If you think you can or can't, you are right.
HENRY FORD

Change your thoughts and you change your world.
NORMAN VINCENT PEALE

Thinking is the hardest work there is--which is
probably the reason so few engage in it.
HENRY FORD

You see things and you say, "Why?" But I dream
things that never were and I say, "Why not?"
GEORGE BERNARD SHAW

Our life is what our thoughts make it. *B.C. FORBES*

That which you vividly imagine, sincerely believe,
ardently desire and enthusiastically act upon will
inevitably come to pass. *WILLIAM R. LUCAS*

All that a man achieves and all that he fails to
achieve is the direct result of his own thoughts.
JAMES ALLEN

Encourage the presence of the positive emotions
as the dominating thoughts in one's mind,
and discourage the presence of all the destructive
emotions. The mind is a creature of habit.
It thrives upon the dominating thoughts fed it.
Through the faculty of will-power, one may
discourage the presence of any emotion, and
encourage the presence of any other. Control of the
mind, through the power of will, is not difficult.
Control comes from persistence and habit.
NAPOLEON HILL

Our aspirations are our possibilities.
ROBERT BROWNING

To think is to differ. *CLARENCE DARROW*

It's amazing what ordinary people can do if they set
out without preconceived notions.
CHARLES F. KETTERING

If you are not a thinking man, to what purpose are
you a man at all? *SAMUEL TAYLOR COLERIDGE*

The happiness of your life depends upon the quality
of your thoughts. *MARCUS AURELIUS*

If you think you are beaten, you are,
If you think you dare not, you don't.
If you like to win, but you think you can't,
It is almost certain you won't.
If you think you'll lose, you're lost,
For out in the world we find,
Success begins with a fellow's will--
It's all in the state of mind.

If you think you are outclassed, you are,
You've got to think high to rise,
You've got to be sure of yourself before
You can ever win a prize.

Life's battles don't always go
To the stronger or faster man,
But soon or late the man who wins
Is the man WHO THINKS HE CAN!
ANONYMOUS

SECURITY

There is only one form of security we can attain
during our lives. It's inner security---the kind
that comes from courage, experience, ability
and willingness to learn, to grow, and to
attempt the unknown. *EARL NIGHTINGALE*

Take a moment to list your friends, relatives,
acquaintances or colleagues who you feel are secure.
Then, make a list of the common attributes they
possess.

What did you find? First, that your list was surprisingly small. Second, that the most common characteristic of those secure people is that they probably are experts in their chosen professions. They are professionals in a world of amateurs. They are excellent at what they do and they know it!

Security is:

- Being a unique person.
- Having uncommon confidence in yourself and your abilities.
- Being an expert at what you do.

Security is not outside of you, in terms of worldly possessions. Security is inside you in terms of competence, confidence and satisfaction. The best thing about security is once you have it (and only you know whether or not you do) you take it with you everywhere. It is your constant friendly companion. You will never lose it.

SELECTED THOUGHTS ON SECURITY

If money is your only hope for independence,
you will never have it. The only real security
in this world is a reserve of knowledge,
experience and ability. *HENRY FORD*

People who take the time and trouble to develop
themselves as persons, who become excellent at their
work, have the kind of security that lasts a lifetime.
EARL NIGHTINGALE

There is no security in life, just opportunity.
DOUGLAS McARTHUR

PEOPLE

You can get everything in life you want if you will
just help enough other people get what they want.
ZIG ZIGLAR

Our relationships with people are crucial to our success.
Before we discuss how to interact successfully with
people, I have two extremely frustrating expressions
that I must mention. They are:

♦   "most people"
♦   "other people"

Many people place their values and base their
judgments on what "most people" would do.
Fortunately for me, I am an individualist constantly
striving to "do my own thing." Whenever "my own
thing" differed from what my mother thought I should
be doing, she would suggest I act like "most people."
I would excitedly retort: "Don't tell me about 'most
people.' I do not want to be like 'most people.'"

Look around you. Do you want to look, walk, talk,
think or be like "most people?" Emphatically NO! The
vast majority of people have an almost unbroken record
of being wrong most of the time about most things.
Show me what "most people" do and I want to do
exactly the opposite! Horace Walpole said: "Nine-tenths
of the people were created so you would want to be
with the other one-tenth."

Observe "most people." Analyze "most people." Then make your own opinions, judgments and decisions based upon your own experiences, observations, study and research. You will soon discover that if you follow the majority, you will be wrong much of the time.

♦ ♦ ♦ ♦ ♦

Stop being concerned about what "other people" think about you. Human nature wants us to try to please and impress others. We make the effort in many ways: how we dress, where we live, what kind of car we drive, how we comb our hair, what social activities we attend. But your success is based on who and what you are and how you treat other people, not on how you try to impress them superficially.

By "doing your own thing" in your own comfortable manner, you will impress more people naturally and easily than you ever could with the most preconceived effort. As some great sage remarked, "You wouldn't be concerned about what other people think of you if you realized how seldom they do."

Look for the good in "other people." Never say, "She's not my kind of person," or, "That is not my sort of crowd." Every human being has a story and it is usually interesting and informative. Seek it out. You will be stretching your mind, broadening your horizons and making your acquaintances into friends.

♦ ♦ ♦ ♦ ♦

There are six steps to success through people:

♦ Recognition. Recognize people as distinct individuals. Use their names as often as is comfortable. Let them feel and know that you recognize them as unique, important individuals, different from all other people.

♦ Service. Remember, your rewards in life will always be in exact proportion to your service. The more and better your service to others, the greater your rewards, happiness and success.

♦ Gratitude. Always be nice, kind, pleasant and friendly to everyone. Smile and say thank you. Thank your wife for being a wonderful wife. Thank your children for being great kids. Thank your associates for being cooperative. Thank your customers for their business. Thank a stranger for holding open a door.

♦ Security. You can make people feel secure by simply being kind, empathetic, generous, courteous and attentive.

♦ Communication. The best way to communicate is to listen---really listen---to what people are saying. Try to feel what they are feeling. Give them feedback by summarizing what they said so they know you know what they meant.

♦ Stimulation. Give people the opportunity to help, to be of value, to produce, to grow.

♦　♦　♦　♦　♦

Here are two examples, one personal and one business, of how using these concepts will make everyone feel good.

Jenny's fifth grade teacher, Judy, was a terrific professional. She was enthusiastic, positive and challenging. Judy was so good that Jenny couldn't wait for the weekend to end so she could go back to school on Monday! One morning I stopped at school just to tell Judy that I was thrilled that Jenny was in her class and she was really doing a great job. Her reaction was shocking and heartwarming. Her face lit up. She thanked me profusely. She said, "You've just made my day. You have no idea how good that makes me feel."

Obviously, I had improved her well-being, but, as an unintended by-product, I had made myself feel great too. This simple, yet genuine compliment given to someone else gave me a warm, wonderful feeling. Without really trying, I found I could make other people feel good about themselves.

♦　♦　♦　♦　♦

The same attitude works in my business too. Our company's philosophy and objective is to provide our clients with "Financial Peace of Mind." Our clients want safety and no risk. On Monday, October 19, 1987, the Dow Jones Industrial Averages fell over 500 points, the biggest one-day decline in history. The next day, all our clients received this letter:

144

"Congratulations on your sound judgment! You should feel good knowing that your money is in completely guaranteed tax-deferred savings plans.

During these chaotic financial times, when the Dow Jones dropped over 500 points in one day and lost approximately 35% of its total value in two weeks, your money has not shrunk one penny! In fact, it has grown and will continue to grow every day regardless of what happens to the stock market.

All of our programs have been designed specifically to give you Financial Peace of Mind. Isn't it reassuring to know that your accounts enjoy:

Complete Safety of Principal and Interest
High Guaranteed Interest
Significant Tax Benefits

Thanks for your confidence in us."

What did we do?

- We helped almost 3,000 people feel good about themselves and their judgment.
- At a time of great stress and concern, we reassured their "Financial Peace of Mind."
- We thanked them for their confidence in us.

What were the results of this simple, sincere effort to tell our valued clients we were genuinely concerned about their welfare?

- ♦ Numerous calls of appreciation and thanks.
- ♦ Increased respect.
- ♦ Immediate new business.
- ♦ Immeasurable goodwill.

♦ ♦ ♦ ♦ ♦

Andrew Carnegie said, "The deepest principle in human nature is the craving to be appreciated, the desire to be important." Treat everyone with decency, respect and honesty. Look for the good in people. Praise it when you find it. Tell people what they do right and genuinely compliment them. Treat each person as the most important person on earth. Follow these suggestions habitually and people will give you all you could possibly want or need.

FRIENDS

The good man is his own friend. *SOPHOCLES*

I am basically a loner, a person who likes himself, enjoys his own company and does not go out of his way trying to make friends or impress people. But you cannot live in a vacuum. You cannot exist completely on your own.

♦ ♦ ♦ ♦ ♦

It is very important to differentiate between friends and acquaintances. Acquaintances are people we know. Friends are people we enjoy, are completely comfortable with, can talk to and trust implicitly. We all have many acquaintances, but very few friends.

True, loyal and lasting friendships are exceedingly rare and wonderful. If you are fortunate to have them, cherish and nurture them. The natural tendency in relationships is toward eroding attentiveness and sensitivity. Do not ignore or neglect your friends. Work hard to preserve them. Give them all the energy you have.

Be alert to making new friends. No one has too many friends. Making new friends is both interesting and rewarding because new friends bring change and excitement into your life. If you consider yourself to be shy and bashful, if you feel uncomfortable with new people, remember the stranger you are reluctant to meet may be just as reluctant to meet you.

Some words of caution. Do not associate with individuals, or have friends who are chronic complainers, whiners and have negative attitudes. You will start adopting their bad habits and attitudes. Cultivate friendships with positive, enthusiastic, intelligent and cheerful people. Choose your friends carefully. Be sure you associate with the kind of people you would most like to resemble.

Some rules for being liked and making friends:

- ♦ The Golden Rule: Always do unto others as you would have them do unto you. Do good things for other people, things that require time, effort, energy, unselfishness and thoughtfulness.

- ♦ Radiate a genuine interest in other people. Be agreeable and sincere. Recognize their individual importance. Show concern for others without trying to get something in return. Be a person that other people like to have around.

- ♦ Consciously schedule more time for friends and loved ones.

- ♦ Accept people unconditionally for who and what they are. Do so without judgment and without reservation. Do not try to change people. You will not be successful and you will only antagonize them.

- ♦ Admire and compliment people on their good traits and their possessions. It raises their self-esteem and increases their willingness to be cooperative with you. Mark Twain said, "I can live for two months on a good compliment."

SELECTED THOUGHTS ON FRIENDS

The only way to have a friend is to be one.
RALPH WALDO EMERSON

Silence is a true friend that never betrays.
CONFUCIUS

The most I can do for my friend is simply to be his
friend. *HENRY DAVID THOREAU*

It is one of the most beautiful compensations of this
life that no man can sincerely try to help another
without helping himself. *RALPH WALDO EMERSON*

A friend is a person before whom I may think aloud.
RALPH WALDO EMERSON

I never found the companion that was as
companionable as solitude.
HENRY DAVID THOREAU

A true friend never gets in your way unless you
happen to be going down. *ARNOLD GLASGOW*

You can make more friends in two months by
becoming really interested in other people, than you
can in two years by trying to get other people
interested in you. *DALE CARNEGIE*

There is a destiny that makes us brothers. None goes
his way alone. All that we send into the lives of
others comes back into our own. *EDWIN MARKHAM*

I will destroy my enemies by converting them to friends. *MAIMONIDES*

If I accept you as you are, I will make you worse; however, if I treat you as though you are what you are capable of becoming, I help you become that. *JOHANN GOETHE*

The friendships which last are those wherein each friend respects the other's dignity to the point of not really wanting anything from him. *CYRIL CONNOLLY*

Be a friend to yourself, and others will. *SCOTTISH PROVERB*

The way to make a true friend is to be one. Friendship implies loyalty, esteem, cordiality, sympathy, affection, readiness to aid, to help. The real friend is he or she who can share all our sorrows and double all our joys. Radiate friendship and it will return seven-fold. *B.C. FORBES*

A friend is a present you give yourself. *CHINESE PROVERB*

There is only one thing better than making a new friend, and that is keeping an old one. *ELMER C. LETERMAN*

Friend: One who knows all about you and loves you just the same. *ELBERT HUBBARD*

Don't believe your friends when they ask you to be honest with them. All they really want is to be maintained in the good opinion they have of themselves. *ALBERT CAMUS*

PARENTS/CHILDREN

It is very tough to be either a parent or a child. So the more we can do to make these tough jobs easier, the happier and smoother life will be for everyone. This chapter is divided into three parts:

- ◆ Your parents.
- ◆ You as a parent.
- ◆ Your children.

YOUR PARENTS

Unfortunately, many people have a tendency to think negatively about their parents. No matter how bad you think your parents were, they probably performed a lot of good, too. They fed, clothed, educated and loved you. They were instrumental in getting you to where you are now. They cannot be all bad.

As I have emphasized before, you must accept the fact that today you are precisely where you have chosen to be in life. As Wayne Dyer says in his book, <u>What Do You Really Want for Your Children?</u>

"You are the sum total of the choices you have made in life. Even if you think your parents made mistakes with you, accept the fact that they were human beings doing what they knew how to do at the time, given the unique conditions of their lives. How can you ask any more of anyone? Forgive them and make peace with everyone in your past, and provide your children with an example of a person who blames no one."

◆ ◆ ◆ ◆ ◆

Often I hear people say, "He's the way he is because when he was little his mother did such and such," or "She's the way she is because as a baby her father did this or that."

Those statements may be absolutely true. And, yes, those parental actions did have an impact and an influence. But, those historical actions are not the overriding cause of what a person is today. Years, even decades, have passed. Other opportunities, experiences and influences have come and gone. Children have grown to be adults.

◆ ◆ ◆ ◆ ◆

Your past is over and cannot be changed. You can remember it, love it, or hate it and wish it had been different. But all the wishing and blaming in the world will not change it. You have to say to yourself, "That is what happened in the past. I may not like it, but I cannot change it. Here is where I am in life today. Where do I want to be tomorrow, next week and next year? Now, how do I go about getting there?"

Being a good parent is one of the world's most difficult jobs, exceeded in difficulty only by the process of growing up itself. Parenting is a task for which you have no real training. You may think you know the responsibilities you are accepting before you become a parent, but I surely didn't. In the seventeenth century, John Welmist, the Earl of Rochester, wrote: "Before I got married I had six theories about bringing up children; now I have six children and no theories."

Parenting is a more complex, time-consuming, expensive job than any gainful employment imaginable. Most of us approach this difficult task with no more understanding and foresight than a simple resolution to try to do a better job with our children than our parents did with us.

The best way to be a good parent has not changed with the ages: It is to set a good example, to be the kind of person your kids can respect and admire. Here are three suggestions that should make parenting a pleasant, wonderful experience and help your children develop into happy, purposeful adults.

♦ Relax. When your child is born, realize that eventually your infant will learn to talk, walk, sleep through the night, become toilet trained, etc. etc. All children need to, and will, develop at their own pace. They do not have to be "the first," "the smartest," the "most musical," the "most athletic," the "most popular" all rolled into one. Do not push or force them. Be "with" them, rather than "at" them. Allow them to enjoy their all too short childhood.

♦ Enjoy them. Just as you should allow your kids to enjoy their own childhood, you should allow yourself to enjoy it too. Your child only grows up once. Savor every moment. Cherish each day, each age. Childhood ends far too quickly. You think you will remember each of their wonderful childhood moments. You will not. There are too many of them and they fly by far too quickly. Keep a diary. Take pictures. Take videos. There are many things in life at which you have many chances. Watching your kids grow up isn't one of them. Do not miss it.

♦ Let your kids be themselves. You have the right to "do your own thing." They should have the same right too. They need to develop at their own pace. They do not need any pushing from you. By the time they get to college, they will not embarrass themselves, or you, with dirty diapers simply because they were not the first kid on the block to be toilet trained.

♦ ♦ ♦ ♦ ♦

The children who are appreciated for what they are, even if they are homely, clumsy, slow, or lazy, will grow up with confidence in themselves--secure and happy. They will have a spirit that will allow them to make the best of all their capacities and their opportunities.

Dr. Benjamin Spock, the author of the "bible" on parenting, <u>Baby and Child Care</u>, wrote: "Love and enjoy your children for what they are, for what they look like, for what they do, and forget about the qualities they do not have..."

Dr. Barney Katz said: "For a healthy inner emotional life, your child must think well of himself, and he cannot do that unless others---above all his parents, who represent the whole world to him---think well of him, too...If you tell him that he is bad, naughty, lazy or a pest, he will, in time, believe you, for you are grownups, his mother and father, and you must know. If you tell him that he is...capable and can do many fine things, he will also believe you and gain the great satisfaction of feeling worthwhile and important."

No one expects or wants children to dominate our lives or our time. But, give some time completely to children so that they know they have our full and undivided attention and cooperation. Let them know that we consider them important enough to devote a part of our day to them. Time properly devoted can go a long way toward giving them a good start in life and building a friendship that can last a lifetime.

♦ ♦ ♦ ♦ ♦

I frequently hear parents, particularly professional working mothers, say: "I don't give my children quantity time, I give them quality time." Hogwash.

Quality time is quantity time! How do you differentiate between the two?

Here is an example. When Adam was 10, I took him to Pittsburgh for an exciting football weekend. Saturday we saw his favorite college team, the University of Miami, play the University of Pittsburgh in the rain and cold. The game was boring and one-sided. We left early in the third quarter even though his team was winning.

When we returned to the hotel, which was across the street from Pittsburgh's Civic Center, I noticed the circus was in town. I asked Adam, "Would you like to go to the circus?" He said, "Dad, I think I would prefer to stay in the hotel, have room service for dinner and play cards." We enjoyed a great evening.

Sunday, we saw his favorite professional team, the Chicago Bears, play the Pittsburgh Steelers in even worse cold. Once again, the game was boring and one-sided. Once again, we left early in the third quarter even though his team was winning.

What was the highlight of the trip? What do we both remember most vividly? Football? No way! It was Saturday night in the hotel playing cards---something we could have done at home! The "quality" events are long since forgotten. The "quantity" event will never be forgotten!

There is nothing more special, unique, prized and valued than children. They are the greatest things ever produced on earth. It is our influence upon their minds and emotions that will shape their lives. Unfortunately, this awesome responsibility is often overlooked or abused by too many parents who are caught up with their own daily activities, pressures and frustrations.

Children are people, too. They are just small and inexperienced. They often are subjected to parental verbal and physical abuse simply because they are too little and too easily intimidated to retaliate. They are forced to accept whatever comes their way. Such behavior is unfortunate, unfair and unconscionable. Children are entitled to and deserve love and respect. Whenever you are playing with, teaching or disciplining your children, ask yourself, "Is my behavior mature, fair and humane? Would I conduct myself this way if my child were an adult who was 25 years old, 6'6" tall and 270 pounds?"

A key to successful child raising is courtesy. It is showing the little people we love and for whom we are responsible, the common courtesy and respect we show to total strangers. Children should grow up living and knowing courtesy as a matter of course. They should enjoy parents treating each other gently and with respect. Then they will know how to treat their own partners some day. Conscientious parents want their children to be raised knowing the rules for success and happiness. These parents show by example that any job worth doing is worth doing well.

♦ ♦ ♦ ♦ ♦

Do you want your children to do and be the best they can possibly be? Of course. How can you help your children achieve their maximum potential? Wayne Dyer says, "When a child grows up to love himself, to be self-confident, to have high self-esteem, and to respect himself, there are literally no obstacles to his total fulfillment as a human being. Once a strong self-portrait is in place, the opinions of others will never be able to immobilize your child. The young person who feels confident as he approaches a task will not be undone by failure, but instead will learn from it. The child who respects himself will respect others, since you give to others what you have inside to give away and, conversely, you cannot give away what you do not have. Similarly, the young person who has learned to love himself will have plenty of love, instead of hate, to give away."

♦ ♦ ♦ ♦ ♦

Here are nine principles for building self-esteem in your children:

♦   Love them. The greatest gift you can give your children is to love them freely, completely and without question. The children who are not fully accepted by their parents, who have always felt that they were not quite right, will grow up lacking confidence.

♦ Treat each child as a special and unique individual. Let them know you love and respect them as individuals. They should know that they are valuable simply because they exist. They are worthy by definition and their worth is not dependent on their actions or their performances. If you see and treat your children as attractive, important and worthy, then they will believe the same things about themselves.

♦ Listen to them. Talk to them. Find out what they are thinking, what they are interested in and what is bothering them. Often it is amazing how much they keep inside. They have problems, concerns and worries of which we are not usually aware. They need our help, our encouragement, our love and our support. Just knowing that we are there, should they have a problem, will give them a tremendous source of comfort and courage.

♦ Provide praise, not criticism. Most parents tend to be quick to criticize, slow to praise. Be positive. Look for the best. Praise your children for taking risks, for attempting the task even if they are unsuccessful.

♦ Discipline them. Children absolutely need and want firm guidelines, reasonable rules and acceptable limits. Undisciplined children are like untrained pets---obnoxious. You are doing your child a great disservice if you do not insist on discipline and manners. The simple way to establish proper, consistent discipline is to reward good behavior, punish poor behavior.

When disciplining, do not discipline in anger and do not use threats. Threats undermine discipline. Let children know, in no uncertain terms, that you will not tolerate unacceptable behavior. Never tell your children they are bad people. Instead, tell them they are wonderful people but exhibiting unacceptable behavior that is not tolerable. Remember to criticize the performance, not the performer.

♦ Educate them. Children need and deserve the best education available. They need to learn to read and write well and to experience the adventure, excitement, love, great ideas and rewards that come from a good education.

♦ Teach them to appreciate and enjoy every day of their lives. Teach them the satisfaction of doing all tasks well, no matter how simple or repetitive they are. It is important that kids understand that something positive can be learned from all of life's experiences. They have to analyze each situation and look for the positive. This technique builds the habit of one success at a time, one day at a time.

♦   Give your children opportunities to make their own decisions and to be responsible. Then support them completely. Instill confidence in their abilities so that they are eager and willing to try new things and not fear failure. Their confidence will grow as they know that you believe in them and trust them.

♦   Teach them to look within themselves for the answers to their questions. Let them have their struggles. Allow them to make their own mistakes. They need to know that whatever is going on inside themselves is up to them.

♦   Teach them that they are responsible for how they use their minds and their bodies. They have control over their own destinies. They can become anything they seriously make up their minds to become. Our job is to help them become it.

♦   Model self-respect. If you want your children to respect themselves, you must provide an unbending example of a person who does the same. Never waiver from that philosophy. Your example as a parent will have a much greater influence on your child than all the talking or all the schooling in the world. The secret is to show them, do not tell them. There is an old adage: "Monkey see; monkey do." The same is absolutely true of children: "Child sees; child does."

161

♦ ♦ ♦ ♦ ♦

It is a wonderful experience when we realize that our children are smarter than we are. They may not be as wise. Wisdom comes with years, if it comes at all. We need to give our children the time, the opportunity and the encouragement to help them understand that they can become anything they seriously make up their minds to become.

SELECTED THOUGHTS ON PARENTS/CHILDREN

The most precious thing a parent can give a child is a lifetime of happy memories. *FRANK TYGER*

Children have neither a past nor a future. Thus they enjoy the present--which seldom happens to us.
JEAN DE LA BRUYERE

The most important thing a father can do for his children is to love their mother.
THEODORE HESBURGH

There are only two things we can give our children. One of them is roots; the other is wings.
CHINESE PROVERB

Children begin by loving their parents. After a time they judge them. Rarely, if ever, do they forgive them. *OSCAR WILDE*

If we had paid no more attention to our plants than we have to our children, we would now be living in a jungle of weeds. *LUTHER BURBANK*

Do not handicap your children by making
their lives easy. *ROBERT HEINLEN*

Some parents give most by giving least.
ARNOLD GLASGOW

Insanity is hereditary. You get it from your children.
LILLIAN HOLSTEIN

If you want children to keep their feet on the ground,
put some responsibility on their shoulders.
ABIGAIL VAN BUREN

Never lend your car to anyone to whom you
have given birth. *ERMA BOMBECK*

WORRY

I have had many troubles in my life, but the
worst of them never came. *JAMES A. GARFIELD*

I have had a long, long life full of troubles, but
there is one curious fact about them--nine-tenths
of them never happened. *ANDREW CARNEGIE*

I am an old man and have had many troubles--most
of which have never happened. *MARK TWAIN*

Of all our troubles great and small, the greatest are
those that don't happen at all. *THOMAS CARLYLE*

These four statements by a United States President, a
great American industrialist, one of America's favorite

163

humorists and a social critic clearly echo the same message: Don't worry!

Don't worry! It is a waste of time and energy. Worry cannot do you any good and it can be very harmful--- mentally, emotionally, psychologically, and physically. Too many people are consumed by needless worry. They permit worry to control their lives, preventing them from enjoying positive, happy, productive, fulfilling lives.

Consider these as reliable estimates of what people worry about:

- ♦ Things that haven't happened yet and probably never will: 40%.
- ♦ Things over and past that cannot be changed by all the worry in the world: 30%.
- ♦ Needless worries about your health: 12%.
- ♦ Petty, insignificant things that are not worth worrying about: 10%.
- ♦ Legitimate situations that deserve your attention and concern: 8%.

Focus your energies on the 8%. Devote yourself to events that are significant and over which you have control, over which you can determine the solutions and the outcomes.

The tragedy of many peoples' lives is that worry robs them of the internal sense that they are competent to cope with the challenges of life and deserving of happiness. They are so consumed and pre-occupied by worry that they do not trust their own minds, instincts, and abilities. They do not feel capable of asserting their own legitimate interests and needs. When the going gets tough, they crumble. They do not persevere because worry has eroded their self-confidence. Because they worry and are insecure and uncertain, they fail more often than they succeed. When they fail, they tell themselves their worry was justifiable and they continue to worry. They get caught in a vicious cycle, a self-fulfilling prophecy of worry, of negative thinking and of failure.

We all make mistakes. That is part of being human. It is perfectly okay to make mistakes. But, once the mistakes are made, learn from them and then forget them. Do not continue to carry them with you as excess, unwanted, very heavy baggage.

Remember, just about all our concerns solve themselves one way or another. Usually, our concerns disappear before they get to us. So you can stop worrying. The sooner you do, the happier you will be. Don't worry!

SELECTED THOUGHTS ON WORRY

Worry - using up your present moments to be consumed about something in the future over which you have absolutely no control. *ANONYMOUS*

Enjoyment of the present is denied to those who worry too much about the future.
WILLIAM FEATHER

Peace of mind: The contentment of the man who is too busy to worry by day, and too sleepy to worry at night. *WOODROW WILSON*

The reason why worry kills more people than work is that more people worry than work. *ROBERT FROST*

Worry is interest paid on trouble before it comes due.
WILLIAM RALPH INGE

There are two days in the week about which I never worry. One is yesterday. The other is tomorrow.
ROBERT JONES BURDETTE

Do not forget the fable of what happened when the Lord, moved by ceaseless complaining, summoned all the people and told them to throw their troubles on one heap. Each one was told to pick out the lightest he could find. And, to the very last man, every one selected his own! *B.C. FORBES*

Put your foot upon the neck of the fear of criticism by reaching a decision not to worry about what other people think, do, or say. *NAPOLEON HILL*

A day of worry is more exhausting than a
day of work. *JOHN LUBBOCK*

Worry never robs tomorrow of its sorrow, but only
saps today of its strength. *A. J. CRONIN*

Worry is evidence of an ill-controlled brain; it is
merely a stupid waste of time in unpleasantness. If
men and women practiced mental calisthenics as they
do physical calisthenics, they would purge their
brains of this foolishness. *ARNOLD BENNETT*

Two things worry most people these days: one, that
things may never get back to normal, and the other,
that they already have. *BITS 'N PIECES*

I am sure that if a coach will follow this
philosophy of life, he will be successful. To
sit by and worry about criticism, which too
often comes from the misinformed or from those
incapable of passing judgment on an individual
or a problem, it is a waste of time. *ADOLPH RUPP*

Fear And Failure

The only people who never fail at anything are those
who don't try anything. *EARL NIGHTINGALE*

It is impossible to go through life without fear, without
mistakes, without failure. Everyone goes through
periods of self-doubt, lack of confidence, fear and
failure. It is as natural as breathing. Successful people
have learned to cope with and overcome these negative
feelings.

The surprising fact is that successful people usually make more mistakes than people who fail. But they also have more successes. They operate on the proven principle that one success can outweigh a hundred failures.

Steve Largent, the former great Seattle Seahawks wide receiver, did not possess outstanding natural assets. Nevertheless, he achieved phenomenal success at a position normally requiring exceptional speed. Here are his comments on failure and his interesting formula for responding to failure:

> "I believe how a person deals with personal failure determines, to a large degree, how successful that person will be. Everyone fails at one time or another, so it's essential to know how to respond to failure.
>
> F - Forget about your failures. Do not dwell on past mistakes.
> A - Anticipate failure. Realize that we all make mistakes.
> I - Intensity should be felt in everything you do. Never be a failure for lack of effort.
> L - Learn from your mistakes. Do not repeat previous errors.
> U - Understand why you failed. Diagnose your mistakes so as not to repeat them.
> R - Respond; do not react to errors. Responding corrects mistakes; reacting magnifies them.
> E - Elevate your self-concept. It is okay to fail, everyone does. Now, how are you going to deal with failure?"

♦ ♦ ♦ ♦ ♦

Every problem, every heartache, every adversity, every failure carries with it the equal opportunity for even greater benefit. To begin to overcome obstacles, you need to rid yourself of indecision, doubt and fear. That requires courage. How do you develop the necessary courage?

♦ The fear of failure is nothing more than a state of mind. And, your state of mind is subject to change, control and direction. Ask yourself: "What great things would I dare to dream and would I undertake if I knew I could not and would not fail?"

♦ Have no fear of failure. Do not sap your energy worrying about failure. Think of failure as one of the necessary steps toward success and accomplishment. Put your energy into the effort needed to succeed.

♦ In a potentially fearful situation, pause, step back and ask yourself what is the worst thing that can happen?

♦ Consider all the alternative solutions.

♦ Be decisive. Make a commitment to your plan of action. Act boldly and enthusiastically. Unseen forces will come to your aid.

♦ Think positively. Project success in your mind. Think success. Visualize your goal as having been attained. As Thoreau said, "Advance confidently in the direction of your dreams." Act as though it were impossible to fail.

♦ Don't give up! Courage requires character and a deep faith in yourself. Persistence is self-discipline in action. Elihu Root said, "Men do not fail. They give up trying."

We all have a tendency to underestimate our own powers, to be uncertain, to feel despair and to consider giving up. As a result, we permit ourselves to fail by passive default rather than run the risk of failing as a result of having made an active effort to succeed. As Henry Ford said: "Failure is only the opportunity to begin again, more intelligently."

SELECTED THOUGHTS ON FEAR AND FAILURE

Most people fail not because they lack intelligence, ability, opportunity or talent but because they haven't given their problem all they've got!
ROBERT H. SCHULLER

Don't be discouraged by a failure. It can be a positive experience. Failure is, in a sense, the highway to success, inasmuch as every discovery of what is false leads us to seek earnestly after what is true, and every fresh experience points out some form of error which we shall afterwards carefully avoid.
JOHN KEATS

Defeat is not the worst of failures. Not to have tried is the true failure. *GEORGE E. WOODBERRY*

When one door closes, another opens; but we often look so long and so regretfully upon the closed door that we do not see the one which has opened for us. *ALEXANDER GRAHAM BELL*

Lack of will power and drive cause more failure than lack of intelligence and ability. *HARRY F. BANKS*

By failing to prepare you are preparing to fail. *BENJAMIN FRANKLIN*

To be successful, you've got to be willing to fail. *FRANK TYGER*

When you make a mistake, there are only three things you should ever do about it: (1) admit it; (2) learn from it, and (3) don't repeat it. *PAUL BRYANT*

Those who try to do something and fail are infinitely better than those who try to do nothing and succeed. *RICHARD BIRD*

Ninety-nine percent of the failures come from people who practice the habit of making excuses. *GEORGE W. CARVER*

Take a chance! All life is a chance. The man who goes farthest is generally the one who is willing to do and dare. The sure-thing boat never gets far from shore. *DALE CARNEGIE*

I cannot give you a formula for success, but I can give you the formula for failure---which is: Try to please everybody. *HERBERT BAYARD SWOPE*

How would you have the thrill of success if you hadn't had the heartache of failure?
MALCOLM FORBES

Both success and failure are largely the results of habit. *NAPOLEON HILL*

Serenity comes not alone by removing the outward causes and occasions of fear, but by the discovery of inward reservoirs to draw upon. *RUFUS M. JONES*

To laugh is to risk appearing the fool.
To weep is to risk appearing sentimental.
To reach out for another is to risk involvement.
To expose feelings is to risk exposing your true self.
To place your ideas, your dreams, before a crowd is to risk their loss.
To love is to risk not being loved in return.
To live is to risk dying.
To hope is to risk despair.
To try is to risk failure.
But risks must be taken, because the greatest hazard in life is to risk nothing.
They may avoid suffering and sorrow, but they cannot learn, feel, change, grow, love, live.
Chained by their attitudes, they are a slave, they have forfeited their freedom.
Only a person who risks is free.
RISKS (AUTHOR UNKNOWN)

Failure can be bought on easy terms; success must be paid for in advance. *CULLEN HIGHTOWER*

The one permanent emotion of the inferior man is fear--fear of the unknown, the complex, the inexplicable. What he wants beyond everything is safety. *H. L. MENCKEN*

8

ATTRIBUTES TO CULTIVATE

ENTHUSIASM

Nothing great was ever achieved without enthusiasm.
RALPH WALDO EMERSON

The word enthusiasm comes from the Greek word, "entheos" which means "the god within." Enthusiasm is one of your greatest assets. It is more important than money, power or influence. Enthusiasm is energy, direction, purpose and commitment. With properly directed enthusiasm, you can acquire anything you seriously want. Happy, successful people have learned to think enthusiastically, act enthusiastically and be enthusiastic. Enthusiastic people are in control of their lives. The few people who are enthusiastic make a difference to both themselves and to others. They create and maintain enthusiasm, their personal "God within."

All great achievements have enthusiasm as the foundation. Look at any successful business, organization or person and you will find people consumed with a specific goal, absolute confidence in their abilities and faith in the purpose of their endeavors. These people are committed to something in which they find enjoyment, challenge and deep satisfaction in achievement.

Enthusiasm, zest and vitality are contagious. If you act enthusiastically, you will be enthusiastic. You will easily develop your own powers and capabilities. You will overcome any tormenting inner doubts. You will create and perfect an unusual aura, a faith that will inspire you and those around you.

♦ ♦ ♦ ♦ ♦

Your enthusiasm is directly proportional to your excitement for what you are doing and for what you look forward to doing. You must enjoy and be excited and thrilled about what you do. Otherwise you will not do it well, fully or successfully.

If you are not doing, for at least part of your life, something that consumes you with excitement and enthusiasm, you are probably leading a sad, unhappy, unfulfilling life. The most fortunate people live constantly energized lives with controlled and balanced enthusiasm. They never lose their enthusiasm. They never lose their zest for what they are doing.

♦ ♦ ♦ ♦ ♦

There are two keys to creating and maintaining enthusiasm:

- ♦ Learning
- ♦ Accomplishment

Learning new things is creative and challenging. It tends to keep your enthusiasm high. Watch children. You will see that they are naturally enthusiastic and naturally happy. Why? Because they are exposed to new and different ideas. They are constantly expanding their worlds. They are always learning.

Adults tend to lose a lot of their enthusiasm for life. They frequently stop learning, stop growing and stop accomplishing. When you fail to explore and get excited about the possibilities open to you, you then join the majority, the people who are tip-toeing safely through life with no challenges, risks, excitement, enthusiasm or accomplishment.

When the enthusiasm goes out of your life, you do not have much left. Life becomes dull in your mind. You lose energy. But you do not have to get lethargic, complacent, tired and bored. Get absolutely enthralled in something, something that you want very badly, something that is worth more than the time and effort required to accomplish it. Throw yourself into it with enthusiastic abandon. The key word is want. It has to be something you want very much to do, as opposed to those jobs, duties and projects you have to do whether you like them or not.

SELECTED THOUGHTS ON ENTHUSIASM

The key to success is not through achievement, but through enthusiasm. *MALCOLM FORBES*

177

If the only thing we leave our children is the quality of enthusiasm, we will have given them an estate of incalculable value. *THOMAS EDISON*

If you can give your son only one gift, let it be enthusiasm. *BRUCE BARTON*

The worst bankrupt person---one who has lost his enthusiasm. *THOMAS CARLYLE*

Ambition is enthusiasm with a purpose.
FRANK TYGER

We act as though comfort and luxury were the chief requirements of life, when all that we need to make us really happy is something to be enthusiastic about.
CHARLES KINGSLEY

The successful don't lose their enthusiasm, don't lose their zest for what they're doing.
MALCOLM FORBES

No person who is enthusiastic about his work has anything to fear from life. *SAM GOLDWYN*

Anyone can succeed if he will only get enthusiastic about life even when life seems empty.
ROBERT H. SCHULLER

If you aren't fired with enthusiasm, you'll be fired with enthusiasm. *VINCE LOMBARDI*

A man doesn't need brilliance or genius; all he needs is energy. *ALBERT M. GREENFIELD*

CREATIVITY/IMAGINATION

Anybody can do anything that he imagines.
HENRY FORD

Creativity and imagination are frequently thought to be uncommon attributes of only a gifted few. That is not true. Creativity and imagination are a part of everyone's natural assets. They are as much a part of you as your mind, heart, arms and legs. You have a vast storehouse of both creativity and imagination. It is up to you to discover, uncover and utilize them.

Utilizing your creativity requires discipline, concentrated effort and hard work. Creative people are alive, awake, eager. They are making progress, learning, producing and thinking. They enjoy their efforts because they give them pleasure and satisfaction.

♦ ♦ ♦ ♦ ♦

Emerson said, "Imitation is suicide." If you are satisfied to compete and/or imitate, you must be satisfied to be just average. You will achieve and earn the same returns and the same rewards as everyone else. You will never be any better than average. So, here is a wonderful rule to follow: "Create, don't compete." If you create, the sky is the limit.

♦ ♦ ♦ ♦ ♦

Work hard to stimulate and develop your innate creativity and imagination. Look at everything as a

179

challenge. Look for new alternatives and new combinations for simple and ordinary things. Look at the familiar as unusual and ask yourself, how can I improve this situation? How can I make it just a little bit better?

Here are five points to remember about creativity:

♦ Because people will always have unmet wants, needs and desires, there are unlimited opportunities for creativity, imagination and innovation. Look for new ways to give people what they want.

♦ You do not have to invent or create anything brand new, unique or dramatic to be successful or to make a fortune. All you have to do is be 10% newer or better in any field. So, look for small, yet effective ways to improve what is already being done. Do it better, faster, easier or cheaper. Here is an excellent example. I was recently reading the label on a Minute Maid Apple Juice can. It said: "Shake gently before enjoying." The use of the word "enjoying," instead of the word "drinking," was intriguing and memorable. Minute Maid not only wanted me to drink their juice, they expressly asked me to enjoy it! This small language difference had a big impact on me, their customer. From now on, I will attempt to buy Minute Maid products.

◆ Here are four simple ways to stimulate creativity:

  ◆ Think.
  ◆ Learn to trust your intuition.
  ◆ Look for the "Acres of Diamonds" in your current position.
  ◆ Do not be afraid to try.

◆ Creativity favors a prepared mind. Educate yourself by reading, studying, attending seminars and listening to tapes. You will become excited and increase your chances of unlocking your innate creative genius.

◆ Learn from your mistakes and failures. They contain valuable hidden lessons. When things go bad, when adversity strikes, always ask yourself: "What can I learn from this situation? How can I make it positive? How can I make lemonade out of this lemon?"

◆ ◆ ◆ ◆ ◆

How do you maximize your own creativity? Here are six ideas:

◆ Approach the situation as though there is a simple solution waiting to be uncovered. Assume there is a logical answer and work hard to find it.

- Clearly define the situation in writing. Take a fresh piece of paper and write the question at the top.

- Use positive ideas and language. Don't tell yourself you have a problem. Tell yourself you possess an exciting, challenging opportunity.

- List all possible solutions.

- Make a decision. Select the one solution you feel is the best and begin to implement it immediately. You have created clarity, focus and energy.

- Set a deadline for completion.

Now you have created a specific goal and timetable for its attainment. Intensely desired goals help you focus your energy and your efforts. Look upon your newly found creative abilities as the means to get from where you are now to where you want to be.

♦ ♦ ♦ ♦ ♦

Imagination is a sign of eternal youthfulness in any person---young or old. Keeping your imagination active will help you stay young in everything but years. People who really achieve greatness make an imaginative, creative, visionary leap into the future. They create a vision, a goal, in their own mind. Then they commit themselves to its achievement and they do not give up until it has become a reality.

SELECTED THOUGHTS ON CREATIVITY/IMAGINATION

Imagination is more important than knowledge.
ALBERT EINSTEIN

There is nothing more powerful than an idea whose time has come. *VICTOR HUGO*

Successful people are dreamers who have found a dream too exciting, too important to remain in the realm of fantasy. *EARL NIGHTINGALE*

Imagination is the key to motivation.
RENE DESCARTES

Wise men put their trust in ideas and not in circumstance. *RALPH WALDO EMERSON*

Of all our faculties, the most important one is our ability to imagine. Can you imagine how it would be not to be able to imagine? *WILT CHAMBERLAIN*

It is better to create than to be learned; creating is the true essence of life. *REINHOLD NIEBUHR*

The power of accurate observations is commonly called cynicism by those who have not got it. *GEORGE BERNARD SHAW*

The rewards in business go to the man who does something with an idea. *WILLIAM BENTON*

183

I am an eternal optimist. I dream; I imagine; my
imagination is never ending. I can see things that I
want and will always want and probably never get.
But it doesn't stop me from wanting and wanting to
try to accomplish those things. *ARNOLD PALMER*

TRUTH AND HONESTY

This above all: to thine own self be true, and it must
follow as the night the day, thou canst not then be
false to any man. *WILLIAM SHAKESPEARE*

Truth and honesty are absolutely essential ingredients
for success. It has been said that if honesty and truth
did not already exist, they should be invented as the
surest way to lasting success and a happy, peaceful
existence.

Truth and honesty are the core of your philosophical
existence, an unchangeable part of you. They are a way
of life. They are a part of everything you say or do. It
is simply saying: "If it isn't honest and truthful, I will
not have anything to do with it."

Truth and honesty are not the best policies, they are the
only ones. Absolute truth and honesty have dramatic
effects:

♦　　They provide you with a euphoric inner
　　　feeling of well-being and security.

♦　　They are sincere and so refreshing that they
　　　effectively build other people's faith and
　　　confidence in you. These attributes are so

unusual that they give you an almost mystical reverence.

♦ ♦ ♦ ♦ ♦

The insurance business is historically characterized as high pressure agents selling whatever they can--- whether or not it serves their clients' best interests. Our business takes the exact opposite approach. We derive success and satisfaction when we advise people not to do or to buy something.

Here is an example. A client's wife was anticipating withdrawing her money from her former employer's retirement plan. He asked me into which annuity programs his wife should deposit the money? I suggested that the best option was to just leave the money where it was. He was shocked that I would give him advice that would not result in increasing my own business.

He was correct---in the short run. But, in the long run, I will receive both his personal business and his company's business. Most importantly, by being absolutely truthful and honest, I had given myself a marvelous feeling of good will and self-satisfaction. I had done the right thing.

♦ ♦ ♦ ♦ ♦

Does this philosophy always work successfully? No. Here is a painful example. Our company was the insurance broker for a large school district's employee benefit program. We received the normal agent commission as compensation. In analyzing these commissions, we thought they were excessive. We were making too much money!

We proposed a fee-paid consulting arrangement eliminating agent commissions. This idea would reduce our compensation and save the district $12,000! With assurances from the Superintendent that, "you take care of us and we will take care of you," we proceeded to change their insurance carriers. These changes resulted in annual savings to the district of $700,000! When we submitted our modest $18,000 bill, the district refused to pay. Rather than creating a lengthy, expensive and stressful lawsuit, we simply accepted their paltry offer of $2,500 as full payment.

In this situation, doing the right thing backfired. I felt foolish, used and abused. Nevertheless, I still sleep very comfortably every night and feel good inside knowing that I did the right thing for what is now my former client!

SELECTED THOUGHTS ON TRUTH AND HONESTY

Honesty is the best policy because it has
so little competition. *ARNOLD GLASGOW*

In dealings between man and man, truth, sincerity
and integrity are of the utmost importance to the
felicity of life. *BENJAMIN FRANKLIN*

We don't see things as they are, we see
things as we are. *UNKNOWN*

UNCOMMON ATTRIBUTES

CHARACTER

Character is your basic being, your attitude, your standards, your ideals, what you think and feel inside. You cannot really define it, but you know inside what kind of a "character" you are.

John Wooden, college basketball's most revered coach, was not only a great coach, but a great teacher. He instilled his philosophy of life in his players. About character he said, "Be more concerned with your character than your reputation, because your character is what you really are, while your reputation is merely what others think you are." Your reputation is precious, but your character is priceless.

SELECTED THOUGHTS ON CHARACTER

I care not what others think of what I do, but I care very much about what I think of what I do: That is character! *THEODORE ROOSEVELT*

The measure of a man's real character is what he would do if he knew he would never be found out. *THOMAS MACAULAY*

Mental toughness is essential to success. Its' qualities are sacrifice and self-denial. Also, most importantly, it is combined with a perfectly disciplined will that refuses to give in. It's a state of mind--you could call it character in action. *VINCE LOMBARDI*

187

The virtue of a man ought to be measured, not
by his extraordinary exertions, but by his
every day conduct. *BLAISE PASCAL*

COURAGE

Of all the college courses I ever took, the best, most
memorable one was Football Coaching, taught by the
late Eddie Finnigan. I do not remember much about
coaching football, but I will always remember Eddie's
overriding, personal philosophy: "It is easy to be
ordinary, but it takes real courage to excel."

It takes courage to stand by your convictions when all
those around you have no convictions. It takes courage
to know what you feel and to live honestly and
truthfully in unbending accordance with those feelings.
It takes courage to stick to your plan and to the
unrelenting pursuit of your goal when you encounter
severe obstacles.

SELECTED THOUGHTS ON COURAGE

The rarest courage is the courage of thought.
ANATOLE FRANCE

The secret of happiness is freedom, and
the secret of freedom is courage.
PERICLES

Courage is the first of the human qualities because
it is the quality which guarantees all others.
WINSTON CHURCHILL

CLASS

What is class? It is easier to recognize class than to define it. Elements of class include humility, poise, confidence and pride. Class is being compassionate, understanding, taking responsibility for yourself and being considerate of the consequences your actions have on others.

Class is confidence. It never runs scared. It is the absolute knowledge that you can meet life head-on and handle whatever comes along. If you have class, you have one of the intangible assets that few possess.

COMMON SENSE

Common sense is something you either have or you do not. If you have to be told what it is, chances are excellent you do not have it! And, if you do not have it, I do not think anyone can tell you how to get it.

SELECTED THOUGHTS ON COMMON SENSE

All the education and all the knowledge in the world can't help the poor soul who has no common sense. *BENJAMIN FRANKLIN*

Nothing astonishes men so much as common sense and plain dealing. *RALPH WALDO EMERSON*

Common sense is genius dressed in its working clothes. *RALPH WALDO EMERSON*

Common sense is uncommon. *JOAN WILLIAMS*

Common sense is instinct. Enough of it is genius.
GEORGE BERNARD SHAW

The wisdom of the wise is an uncommon degree
of common sense. WILLIAM R. INGE

Common sense in an uncommon degree is what
the world calls wisdom.
SAMUEL TAYLOR COLERIDGE

Common sense and good nature will do a lot to
make the pilgrimage of life not too difficult.
W. SOMERSET MAUGHAM

One pound of learning requires ten pounds of
common sense to apply it. PERSIAN PROVERB

Common sense is the knack of seeing things as
they are, and doing things as they ought to be done.
CALVIN STOWE

One of the great maladies of our time is the
way sophistication seems to be valued above
common sense. NORMAN COUSINS

The three great essentials to achieve anything
worthwhile are first, hard work; second,
stick-to-itiveness; third, common sense.
THOMAS EDISON

Common sense is the innate instinct and ability to
know when, where and how to act and react.
ANONYMOUS

COMMUNICATING: LISTENING AND TALKING

A gossip is one who talks to you about others;
a bore is one who talks to you about himself;
and a brilliant conversationalist is one who
talks to you about yourself. *LISA KIRK*

We are all so eager to impress other people with our thoughts knowledge and expertise, to solve other people's problems, and to hear ourselves talk, that we spend far too much time and energy talking and far too little time listening.

Successful people tend to be good listeners. They know they will rarely make a mistake when they talk less and listen more. As with all other worldly skills, you can learn to be a good listener and to inspire others to speak freely.

Whose conversational abilities do you respect and admire? What characteristics and attributes do successful people possess? The answer is probably two-fold:

- They listen more than they talk.
- They get you to talk about yourself. They ask questions: How are you? What do you think about various current issues? How are your children?

When the conversation is over, you think to yourself: "Isn't that a wonderful, smart, pleasant, happy, cheerful person?" She may well be, but you probably don't really know it. She has made you feel wonderful, smart, pleasant, happy and cheerful by keeping her mouth shut and letting you:

- Talk about yourself.
- Express your feelings.
- Show your knowledge about a variety of subjects.
- Propose your simple solutions to most of the world's pressing problems.

We confuse talking with communicating. Talking is one-sided. Talking "to" is not communicating "with." Communicating requires a balance of talking and listening. Good conversation should be like a game of tennis, with each person getting his turn at the ball, not like a game of golf, where one person just keeps on hitting his own ball until the game is over.

Why don't people listen? Probably because they think, "What have you got to offer me?" It is plain rude to be talking with someone and, at the same time, be completely tuned out to what they are saying. Listening is more than just hearing the words. It is aggressively listening for clues to what the person is really trying to say. It is concentrating 100% on what the other person is saying.

To become a good listener, follow these principles:

192

- ◆ Face speakers directly. Look them in the eye.
- ◆ Listen attentively, quietly and patiently.
- ◆ Listen without interruption and without thinking about what you are going to say when the speaker stops.
- ◆ Pause before replying. You actually hear better when you pause before responding and you will know the other person has finished his point.
- ◆ Feed it back in your own words. This makes it clear to the other person that you listened carefully and fully understood what was said.
- ◆ For clarification, ask open-ended questions--- what, where, when, how, who, why?
- ◆ For commitment, ask close-ended questions that must be answered yes or no.
- ◆ Always be conscious of your listen/talk ratio. Regulate and control both for the delicate balance good communication requires.

◆ ◆ ◆ ◆ ◆

There are many practical implications of good listening and good communication. Among them:

- ◆ Your relationships with your children. How often have you heard youngsters say, "My parents don't understand me." Understanding is not the basic problem. More likely, parents do not listen to their children, to their wants, desires, problems, emotional concerns. Parents spend too much time telling their children what to do and not enough time listening to them.

193

- ♦ Your business success. It has been estimated that 75% of your income depends upon your communication skills. Think about it. Who are the successful, high-earning people? Doctors, lawyers, business leaders, people who are well-educated, articulate communicators.

- ♦ Your own daily feeling of well-being. Try this exercise in communication. Never let a day go by without seeing, recognizing and commenting about the nice things people do around you---be it your wife, your children, your colleagues or someone you do not even know. Certainly someone does or says something good that deserves recognition. Take the few seconds necessary to say "thank you."

You do not have to be unduly flattering or obsequious. You are not looking for anything in return. You are just being honest and decent to a fellow human being who is bound to appreciate your small act of kindness.

♦ ♦ ♦ ♦ ♦

Learn to be an effective communicator. It is one of the most important things you can do to insure success.

SELECTED THOUGHTS ON COMMUNICATING: LISTENING AND TALKING

The less men think, the more they talk.
MONTESQUIEU

I like to listen. I have learned a great deal from
listening carefully. Most people never listen.
ERNEST HEMINGWAY

Why did God give man two ears and one mouth? So
that he will hear more and talk less. *LEO ROSTEN*

Speaking or writing without thinking is
like shooting without aiming.
ARNOLD GLASGOW

All wise men share one trait in common:
the ability to listen. *FRANK TYGER*

Silence is one of the hardest arguments to refute.
JOSH BILLINGS

People are too anxious to hear themselves talk,
and if they've made what they perceive to
be a brilliant point, they're too anxious to
repeat it, rephrase it and beat it to death.
MARK McCORMICK

There are few people who don't become
more interesting when they stop talking.
MARY LOWEY

It is all right to hold a conversation, but you
should let go of it now and then.
RICHARD ARMOUR

The older I grow, the more I listen to people who
don't say much. *GERMAIN GLIDDEN*

Quiet persons are always welcome.
THOMAS FULLER

SELF-ESTEEM AND CONFIDENCE

Of all the judgments that we pass in life, none is as important as the one we pass on ourselves, for that judgment touches the very center of our existence.
NATHANIEL BRANDON

Esteem means "to appreciate the worth of." So self-esteem means to appreciate ourselves. It is confidence in our own basic ability to:

♦ Cope with the challenges and opportunities of life.
♦ Trust our own mind and judgment.
♦ Instill in ourselves the belief and feeling that we are worthy of happiness.

Self-esteem is not derived from the things you have done, the objects you possess or what other people think of you. Your own happiness and self-esteem are what <u>you</u> determine them to be. They are inside of you, not outside.

It is amazing how many people go through life without ever recognizing that their feelings toward other people are largely determined by their own feelings toward themselves. If you're not comfortable with yourself, you can't be comfortable with others. If you do not respect yourself, you cannot respect others. If you do not love yourself, you will not be able to love others.

Your self-esteem and your attitude help determine how high in life you will rise emotionally, spiritually, creatively and financially. Self-esteem is truly a self-fulfilling prophecy. It establishes your entire set of expectations, either happy or sad, good or bad, positive or negative. You then proceed to turn your perceptions and thoughts into realities by the way you act.

Your self-esteem is determined by how much you believe yourself to be valuable, worthwhile, important, and competent. It arises from a true sense of competence, a supreme confidence in yourself. You think and act in a manner consistent with your own innermost convictions. You soon discover that the more confidence you have, the less you will be bothered or even concerned with critics. You will reach a peak point where you will not even listen to them. You will not care what people say about you because inside yourself, you know the absolute truth about yourself.

♦ ♦ ♦ ♦ ♦

Winners are people who every day go out and do things that make them feel better about themselves. They successfully perform little insignificant acts that build a habit and foundation of success. These small successes build their confidence into a large indestructible force. There are old bromides that say:

♦   "You give a man a fish and he eats for a day. You teach a man to fish and he eats for a lifetime."

♦   "I hear, I forget. I see, I remember. I do, and I understand."

Building and achieving self-esteem and confidence require action and accomplishment. To gain confidence, Just Do It, Just Do It, Just Do It. Confidence enables you to perform up to your capabilities without holding back and without the fear of failure.

♦ ♦ ♦ ♦ ♦

Bryant Gumbel, the successful TV sportscaster turned host of NBC television's Today show, says:

"I've always found that the greatest obstacle to success is one's ability to depress himself. It's easy and it's natural. You see the disorder in the world, take note of the long road ahead, calculate its difficulty and figure there is no way you will ever hook up with success.

My formula to combat that is quite simple. You start by knowing yourself and by giving yourself credit for the real abilities you have. The people who are what you'd like to be are not, in most cases, innately superior. Having properly evaluated yourself, you begin your road up exactly as you climb stairs---one at a time. Do not look at the top of the stairs and moan how far up it is! Just know it's there and start climbing. With each step, you

198

will find your self-esteem growing and your pace quickening. Soon, that top of the stairs will appear to be reaching for you as quickly as you are reaching for it.

Through it all, remember---nothing is given away! What you get, you earn with diligence and intelligence. It's amazing how lucky you get after working on something long after others have given up. Success---it's easier than you think!"

One of my strongest recollections of building my own self-confidence came when I ran for President of Shaker Heights High School student body. Each candidate had to give a speech to the entire student body. I was very nervous sitting on the stage watching all my fellow students file into the auditorium. I vividly recall looking at the other candidates and saying to myself:

- ◆ I am the best candidate. I should be President.
- ◆ All these people are here to listen to me. If they thought they could do better, they would be up on this stage.
- ◆ Take a deep breath, relax and give your speech with enthusiasm, strength and sincerity.

I did and I won.

My thinking process here was not a one time phenomenon. I have used this same logic and rationale many times in succeeding years. You have to keep telling yourself:

- No one is better than I am. (Remember Mohammed Ali's constant theme: "I am the greatest!" He believed in himself and soon had the entire world---including his opponents---believing it.)
- I can achieve whatever I set out to do.
- It is impossible to fail.

SELECTED THOUGHTS ON SELF-ESTEEM AND CONFIDENCE

Self-trust is the first secret of success.
RALPH WALDO EMERSON

What a man thinks of himself, that is what determines, or rather, indicates, his fate.
HENRY DAVID THOREAU

The great thing in the world is to know how to be sufficient unto oneself. *MICHAEL DE MONTAIGNE*

I begin to understand that the promises of the world are, for the most part, vain phantoms, and that to have faith in oneself and become something of worth and value is the best and safest course.
MICHELANGELO

Confidence is that feeling by which the mind embarks on great and honorable courses with a sure hope and trust in itself. *CICERO*

Know and believe in yourself, and what others think won't disturb you. *WILLIAM FEATHER*

To conquer oneself is the best and noblest victory. *PLATO*

We know what we are, but know not what we may be. *SHAKESPEARE*

Life is not easy for any of us. But what of that? We must have perseverance and, above all, confidence in ourselves. We must believe that we are gifted for something, and that this thing, at whatever cost, must be attained. *MARIE CURIE*

There is no feeling in this world to be compared with self-reliance---do not sacrifice that to anything else. *JOHN D. ROCKEFELLER*

When you have confidence, you can have a lot of fun and when you have fun, you can do amazing things. *JOE NAMATH*

Only a person who has faith in himself can be faithful to others. *ERICH FROMM*

9

CAREER

MONEY/RICHES/WEALTH

The real measure of a man's wealth is how much
he would be worth if he lost all his money.
ANONYMOUS

Wealth has nothing to do with accumulation of money.
Wealth is knowledge, confidence, attitude. It is the
security that comes from knowing that no matter what
happens, you can always change your thinking, your
beliefs, your actions, your strategies and succeed.

Adopt this philosophy: "You can take away my cash,
my credit, my financial statements---everything the
world considers wealth. But I will always have the only
thing that really counts: my own natural resources, my
supreme self-confidence, my time, my ability to
communicate, my courage and my knowledge." You do
not have to have any money to be a success.

203

◆ ◆ ◆ ◆ ◆

You should understand that the only people who "make" money work in a mint. Every one else must earn it. Money is the tangible evidence and result of success. The amount of money you earn will always be in direct proportion to the demand for what you do, how well you do it and how difficult you are to replace. That is why trying to get something for nothing does not work.

Becoming rich is really no different than becoming exceptionally good at anything else. It is simply a matter of attitude. Once and for all, you must commit yourself and then stay with it until you eventually achieve what you set out to accomplish. Think of nothing else. Work at it until it becomes a reality.

◆ ◆ ◆ ◆ ◆

There are two ironies about money:

◆ It is only important to the extent that you do not have it.
◆ It eludes you if you seek it directly.

Money, like happiness, is an effect. It is the direct result of your service. If you want to become rich, do not concentrate on getting rich. Instead, find your own special area of interest in which you can focus your dedication and commit your energies. You will experience frustrating times, times when you consider giving up. But you will stick with it because you are dedicated. One day you will be rich---and probably famous, too.

There are three steps to riches:

- ♦ Find a need or want for which there is a demand.
- ♦ Make up your mind that you can do it.
- ♦ Don't give up.

Easy? No, but the process works.

When you study self-made millionaires, you will find that they are not necessarily intellectual giants or geniuses. They are not necessarily smarter than the average person. You will also find that they work hard--12, 14 or 16 hours a day. It is not because they need the money. It is their love of the journey. It is the joy, the pleasure, the satisfaction and the exhilaration that make them winners and make them rich.

As a first step to planning your financial future, you should determine:

- ♦ Your annual income now and how much you want to earn in the future.
- ♦ How much you want in a savings or investment account.
- ♦ How much you want for retirement income.

Most people never decide on any one of these three items, let alone all three. If you make these three decisions, you will have set your course and determined where you are going. If you are serious, you will get there.

You must be absolutely specific about these amounts. It is not acceptable to say, "I want plenty of money." Each financial objective must have a definite sum next to it. Write them on a piece of paper and always carry it with you. When you get up each morning and before you go to bed each night, take out the paper and read it. Think of yourself as already having accumulated those dollars, as already having achieved your goals.

◆ ◆ ◆ ◆ ◆

There is a very simple philosophy for the accumulation of wealth. It is so simple that you may have overlooked it. Your philosophy should be: "Part of all I earn is mine to keep. This is my money that is untouchable."

You should participate in a forced savings or investment program. Payroll deduction is best because it is automatic and works every pay day. Payroll deduction is almost "painless extraction."

Let time and compound interest combine to make you wealthy. Here is a very simple example of how your money accumulates at 6% interest:

No. of Years	Amount Deposited Each Month at 6%		
	$100	$250	$500
5	$ 6,982.40	$ 17,456.00	$ 34,912.01
10	16,326.43	40,816.07	81,632.15
15	28,830.85	72,077.12	144,154.23
20	45,564.58	113,911.44	227,822.88
25	67,958.08	169,895.21	339,790.42
30	97,925.65	244,814.12	489,628.23

How much you must deposit each month at 6% to accumulate:			
Number of Years	$100,000	$250,000	$500,000
10	$ 612.50	$ 1,531.26	$ 3,026.52
15	346.85	867.13	1,734.25
20	219.47	548.67	1,097.34
25	147.15	367.87	735.75
30	102.12	255.30	510.59

The achievement of financial success requires sufficient imagination to see and understand that the accumulation of money cannot be left to chance, good fortune or luck. You must understand that all wealthy people had to dream, hope, plan and work before they acquired their money. Start today, right now. No excuses permitted. Do not wait for the "right time" in your life to begin your systematic savings program. The time will never be just right for you.

♦ ♦ ♦ ♦ ♦

Do not use any of these "Five Ages of Can't" excuses:

Age 21-30 - I can't save now. I am just getting my start in life. I don't make a lot yet, and I am entitled to a little fun while I am young. There is plenty of time. I will wait until I start making a little more. Then I will save.

Age 30-45 - I can't save now. I've got a growing family. Children and a house cost a lot of money. It takes all I have to keep them going. As soon as they are a little older, it'll cost less. Then I will save.

Age 45-55 - I can't save now. I've got two children in college. It is all I can do to pay their expenses. In fact, I had to borrow for their tuition last fall. This is the most expensive period in a person's life. I can't save a penny.

Age 55-65 - I can't save now. I know I should. But things aren't breaking like they were. It is not easy for a person my age to step out and get a better job. I will have to ride along where I am. Maybe something will break.

Age 65 - I can't save now. We're living with my son and his wife. My Social Security doesn't go very far. I wish I had started saving 20 years ago, but it is too late now. You can't save when there is no income.

♦ ♦ ♦ ♦ ♦

Both poverty and wealth are the direct result of thought. Most people wish and hope to be rich. Only a few know that a definite plan plus an unbending commitment for wealth are the only dependable means of assuring your financial success.

♦ ♦ ♦ ♦ ♦

Once you have accumulated all your desired wealth, remember the old adage: "It is good to have money and the things that money can buy, but it is good, too, to check once in a while to make sure you haven't lost the things that you cannot buy."

SELECTED THOUGHTS ON MONEY/RICHES/WEALTH

The greatest wealth you can ever get will be in yourself. *HORACE BUSHNELL*

There is no wealth but life. *JOHN RUSKIN*

We make ourselves rich by making our wants few. *HENRY DAVID THOREAU*

Wealth does not bring excellence, but that wealth comes from excellence. *PLATO*

No man can tell whether he is rich or poor by
turning to his ledger. It is the heart that makes a man
rich. He is rich according to what he is, not
according to what he has. *HENRY WARD BEECHER*

He is a wise man who does not grieve for the things
which he has not but rejoices in those which he has.
EPICTETUS

It's what we value, not what we have, that
makes us rich. *UNKNOWN*

After a certain point, money is meaningless. It's
the game that counts. *ARISTOTLE ONASSIS*

Anyone who says money doesn't buy happiness
doesn't know where to shop. *ANONYMOUS*

There are two times in a man's life when he
should not speculate: when he can't afford it,
and when he can. *MARK TWAIN*

His money is twice tainted: 'taint yours
and 'taint mine. *MARK TWAIN*

Three points to follow in becoming a billionaire:
arise early; work late; strike oil. *J. PAUL GETTY*

Make money the old fashioned way---inherit it!
ANONYMOUS

Do your work---not just your work and no more, but
a little more for the lavishing sake; that little more
which is worth all the rest. And if you suffer, as you
must, do your work. Put your heart into it, and the
sky will clear. Then out of your very doubt and
suffering will be born the supreme joy of life.
DEAN BRIGGS

The great physician Sir William Osler described work
as the "The Master Word." Work brings clarity,
self-respect, satisfaction and usefulness to your life.

Almost all of us must work for a living. And, strange
as it may seem, work is actually beneficial. Why?
Because work gives purpose, meaning and substance to
your life. One of your greatest responsibilities is to find
work that is meaningful to you. You must enjoy what
you are doing. Otherwise, you will not do it
enthusiastically, well or successfully. And when you
find it, you will love doing it. It will fill you with joy
and satisfaction and will bring you all the rewards
(emotional, psychological and financial) that you desire.

♦ ♦ ♦ ♦ ♦

The happiest people almost always are the busiest most
productive people. Usually they are serving other
people in some way. They never take their work for
granted. They love it and find it filled with interest,
excitement and reward. By losing themselves in what
they are doing and where they are going, happiness and
success quietly join them and become a part of them.

Athletes and movie stars are excellent examples. They are engaged in work that comes closest to perfectly matching their natural likes and talents. They are doing that at which they excel. They are in their element and would be doing what they are doing even if they were not earning enormous amounts of money.

♦ ♦ ♦ ♦ ♦

There are no rewards without long hard hours of work. The harder you work, the better, more effective, and more competent you become. For example, the average self-made millionaire works over 60 hours a week. In our society, you work eight hours a day for survival. If you work only eight hours a day, that is all you will do---survive at a subsistence level. Everything you do over eight hours a day is an investment in your future to guarantee your own success.

♦ ♦ ♦ ♦ ♦

One of the greatest mistakes you can make is to think that, no matter what your job, you work for anyone but yourself. Understand, we are all self-employed. We all work for ourselves. The fastest way to move ahead in any organization is to treat the company as if it belongs to you---as if it were your own. Always ask yourself: If you were going to take the stock of your personal company to the public, would you buy stock in yourself?

♦ ♦ ♦ ♦ ♦

You can have one of three attitudes toward your work:

- ♦ You absolutely love what you are doing and would not consider doing anything else for love or money. You are enthusiastic, positive and exuberant about what you do.

- ♦ You tolerate your work as a necessary means to an end---the end being to earn enough money on which to live. You don't really like your work, but you don't hate it either. You would be receptive to a change if a better job came along.

- ♦ You hate your work, dread getting up in the morning and would love to be doing anything else, or better yet, nothing at all.

You know exactly which category you fit into. If you are not in the first group, you need to examine yourself and your situation immediately. Ask yourself, "Is this the kind of work I want for the rest of my life? If not, what kind of career and job do I want? Where will I be next year, the year after, and five years from now?"

You have to develop definitive answers to these questions and set specific goals. You must be certain where you are and where you want to go. It is almost impossible to hit a target you haven't established and cannot see.

If you do not love your job enough to want to be the best at it, if you don't love to get to work in the morning, then you should consider finding something else. Your life work must be much more than just an eight-hour-a-day job. People grow old in occupations with fixed limitations, uninteresting surroundings and no creative demands on their imagination. Old age comes when hope and planning for the future stop. People who have no dreams to spur them on, no goal to achieve, are already old.

◆ ◆ ◆ ◆ ◆

Way back in 1966, Peter Drucker, the management guru, wrote a book called "The Effective Executive." Here are four simple suggestions for learning to improve your job effectiveness:

◆ Train yourself to make good use of your time.

◆ Concentrate on the few major areas where superior performance will produce outstanding results. First things, first; second things not at all.

◆ Build on your strengths. Visualize what you can do, rather than what you cannot do.

◆ Gear your efforts to results, rather than to work.

◆ ◆ ◆ ◆ ◆

For success, always do more than you are paid for and always put more in than you take out. Practice this art of over compensation. Go the extra mile. The fastest track to success is to work harder than anyone else. Consider these three bits of advice:

- ♦ The best preparation for tomorrow is to do today's work extremely well.
- ♦ The harder you work, the more energy you have.
- ♦ The harder you work, the luckier you get.

As Thomas Edison said, "The three great essentials to achieve anything worthwhile are first, hard work; second, stick-to-itiveness; third, common sense."

SELECTED THOUGHTS ON WORK/BUSINESS

Work is a grand cure of all the maladies that
ever beset mankind. *THOMAS CARLYLE*

Work is what we make it, a pain or a pleasure. And
as most of our waking hours are spent at work, it is
the part of wisdom to get on friendly terms with it.
B.C. FORBES

You cannot be successful if you don't love what
you're doing. Whatever really turns you on,
do it. Psychic income is what real income is
used for anyway. *MALCOLM FORBES*

A person who has nothing to do, nothing that he
loves to do, must be pretty miserable. He should
find the work he likes; and when he does, he will
one day realize, all of a sudden, that he's happy.
EARL NIGHTINGALE

If you're doing work you don't like, even the smallest task seems to drag on and on and on; it seems to take forever. Whereas the old cliché about if you're having a good time, time flies, is true. You want to apply this to your workday. *MALCOLM FORBES*

The reward of a thing well done is to have done it.
RALPH WALDO EMERSON

If people knew how hard I have to work to gain my mastery, it wouldn't seem wonderful at all.
MICHELANGELO

Joy in one's work is the consummate tool.
PHILLIPS BROOKS

When you like your work, every day is a holiday.
FRANK TYGER

Ambition, energy, industry, perseverance are indispensable requisites for success in business.
PHINEAS T. BARNUM

Few persons realize how much of their happiness, such as it is, is dependent upon their work, upon the fact that they are kept busy and not left to feed upon themselves. *JOHN BURROUGHS*

Work spares us from three great evils: boredom, vice and need. *VOLTAIRE*

Few of us get anything without working for it.
WILLIAM FEATHER

Success in business hinges mostly on the ability to get the important things done. *WILLIAM FEATHER*

By working faithfully eight hours a day, you may eventually get to be a boss and work twelve hours a day. *ROBERT FROST*

Even if you're on the right track, you'll get run over if you just sit there. *WILL ROGERS*

Until you try, you don't know what you can't do. *HENRY JAMES*

Whenever an individual or a business decides that success has been attained, progress stops. *THOMAS J. WATSON*

For it is the willingness of people to give of themselves over and above the demands of the job that distinguishes the great from the merely adequate organization. *PETER DRUCKER*

Thank God every morning when you get up that you have something to do that day which must be done, whether you like it or not. Being forced to work, and forced to do your best, will breed in you temperance and self-control, diligence and strength of will, cheerfulness and content, and a hundred virtues which the idle never know. *CHARLES KINGSLEY*

It's amazing how much can be accomplished if no one cares who gets the credit. *BLANTON COLLIER*

217

The trouble with complete security is its drab monotony. A life without the impetus of work and struggle is only half a life, and most of us would settle down to complete inertia if we did not have to work to eat. *CID RICKETTS SUMNER*

If we are willing to put the best of ourselves in our present jobs, and are willing to grow slowly, success will come. *WILLIAM FEATHER*

A celebrity is a person who works hard all his life to become well known, then wears dark glasses to avoid being recognized. *FRED ALLEN*

When the joy of the job's gone, when it's no fun trying anymore, quit before you're fired.
MALCOLM FORBES

The big things that come our way are seldom the result of long thought or careful planning, but rather they are the fruit of seed planted in the daily routine of work. *WILLIAM FEATHER*

Don't be afraid to give your best to what seemingly are small jobs. Every time you conquer one it makes you that much stronger. If you do the little jobs well, the big ones will tend to take care of themselves.
DALE CARNEGIE

Work is dull only to those who take no pride in it.
WILLIAM FEATHER

No joy is comparable to that which comes from doing your job well. *WILLIAM FEATHER*

If at first you don't succeed, try hard work.
WILLIAM FEATHER

Experience and judgment must be gained by the slow
process of doing. *WILLIAM FEATHER*

The road to success is rough. You have to pave
it yourself. To set the world on fire, warm up
to your job. *ARNOLD GLASGOW*

There is no future in any job. The future lies in the
man who holds the job. *GEORGE CRANE*

To do today's work well and not to bother about
tomorrow is the secret of accomplishment.
ANONYMOUS

To find a career to which you are adapted by
nature and then to work hard at it, is about as
near to a formula for success and happiness
as the world provides. *MARK SULLIVAN*

In a small business, you always know who the
owners are. They are the ones who answer the
telephones after 5:30. *LOIS WYSE*

To do great work, a man must be very idle as
well as very industrious. *SAMUEL BUTLER*

EXCELLENCE AND QUALITY

The quality of your life will be determined by
the level of your commitment to excellence, no
matter what your chosen field. *VINCE LOMBARDI*

Achieving excellence means making a commitment to excellence. It means making a decision that you are going to be the best at what you do. As long as you demand excellence and accept nothing less, you will assure yourself success because the universal respect for excellence never changes.

Excellence is revered wherever it is found and commands the highest price. People who perform with excellence achieve internal comfort, joy and satisfaction. Their work becomes a major source of accomplishment. They derive deep satisfaction from being uncommon people producing excellent products or services. They achieve a lifetime of internal security. They realize that there is always a market for the best and they never have to worry about their incomes.

Throughout history, great people such as Antonio Stradivari, William Shakespeare, Leonardo da Vinci, and Thomas Chippendale created masterpieces. They performed with excellence not because of any external pressure, but because of their own internal insistence on excellence.

Confucius said, "The nature of man is always the same; it is their habits that separate them." Aristotle said, "Excellence is not an act but a habit." You can develop excellent habits in everything you do.

◆ ◆ ◆ ◆ ◆

Excellence does not mean doing one thing a thousand percent better. It means doing a thousand things one percent better.

In business, the constant and never-ending search for quality should be paramount. People are naturally attracted to quality. It is something everybody wants. It is what people want in their cars, their homes, and everything they buy. And the people who demand excellence in the product they manufacture or the service they provide will succeed sooner or later.

No one ever achieved much in life by doing things in an average way. Anything less than a commitment to excellence is an acceptance of mediocrity. Strive for excellence. Commit to quality in every single detail of your work. Quality will make your work worth doing. This commitment to quality, this demand for excellence, will permeate you. It will give you dignity, your business character and your customers satisfaction.

People remember quality long after they have forgotten price. One of Tom Peters' basic management principles for success is, "There is no limit whatsoever to the amount of quality that can be added to anything. If you believe in the unlimited ability to improve the quality of what you offer, and if you behave with total integrity in your business dealings, then all the rest of that stuff---market share, growth and profitability will take care of itself."

♦ ♦ ♦ ♦ ♦

Every year, thousands of businesses fail, hundreds of thousands of men and women are discharged from their jobs, because they tried to get maximum results from minimum effort. It used to be that when people parted they would say: "work hard." Today, they say: "take it easy." How often have you heard the expression, "I am not going to knock myself out; I do no more than I have to." The people with that philosophy are the poorest people on earth. People who produce less than their very best are cheating. And the only people they are really cheating are themselves.

♦ ♦ ♦ ♦ ♦

Excellence can be attained if you:

- ♦ Care more than others think is wise.
- ♦ Risk more than others think is safe.
- ♦ Dream more than others think is practical.
- ♦ Expect more than others think is possible.

♦ ♦ ♦ ♦ ♦

Achieving excellence is not easy. It is a continuing process that requires commitment and unending hard work. Excellence, like success and happiness, is a journey, not a destination.

SELECTED THOUGHTS ON EXCELLENCE AND QUALITY

Excellence is everything, because mediocrity
is nothing. *JAMES D. DONOVAN*

Whatever is worth doing at all is worth doing well."
LORD CHESTERFIELD

Excellence is rare. It calls attention to itself
wherever it exists. *ANDY ROONEY*

Quality is never an accident; it is always the result of
intelligent effort. *JOHN RUSKIN*

You become well-to-do from doing what
you do well. *FRANK TYGER*

Strive for perfection in everything you do. Take
the best that exists and make it better. When it
does not exist, design it. Accept nothing nearly
right or good enough. *HENRY ROYCE*

Tolerate imperfection in others, never in yourself.
FRANK TYGER

Professionalism means consistency of quality.
FRANK TYGER

The happiness of your life depends upon the
quality of your thoughts. *MARCUS AURELIUS*

Happy, successful, motivated people first expect
excellence from themselves and from everyone
they work with. They dare to dream big dreams,
expect big things. *JOE BATTEN*

SERVICE

Here is a short story by Cavett Robert that shows the unique importance of service.

> One day the King's best personal servant was walking in a dense forest near the palace. There he stumbled and fell down a hill. He awakened, looked around, and found at his feet the proverbial magic cup, which, when rubbed, released a genie.
>
> The genie said, "Your finding this cup was no accident. You have worked hard all your life. So you may make one wish. But make it carefully because you can have only one.
>
> The man replied, "All my life I have been in positions requiring that I serve others. In fact, I am known as 'The Servant of the Kingdom.' In the future, I want people to wait on me and serve me. Yes, that's it. I want the tables turned. I want servants to do everything for me."
>
> Sure enough, when the man returned to the castle, the door was opened for him. His food was cooked, his meals served, his dishes washed, his clothes cared for by others.
>
> He was not allowed to perform his usual work. Everything was done for him.
>
> For the first month, the newness of the experience amused him. The second month, it became

irritating. During the third month, it became unbearable.

So the man returned to the forest and searched until he found the genie again. He said, "I've discovered that having people wait on me isn't as pleasant as I'd thought. I'd like to return to my original station and once again be 'The Servant of the Kingdom.'"

The genie replied, "I am sorry, but I can't help you. I had the power to grant only one wish."

The man said, "But, you don't understand. I want to serve people. I found it far more rewarding to do things for others than to have all those things done for me."

The genie just shook his head.

The man begged, "But you must help me. I'd rather be in hell than not be able to serve others."

The genie said sorrowfully, "My friend, where do you think you have been for the last ninety days?"

Service is the key to success in your working career. Your rewards in life are directly proportional to the service you provide others. First comes the service. Then come the rewards.

You cannot stand in front of a fireplace and say, "Give me heat, then I will put in the wood." How many businesses try his illogical approach saying, "Give us your business, then we will provide you service." The proper attitude is: "Allow us to first serve you so that we can then earn your confidence and your business."

Zig Ziglar's philosophy is: "You can get anything you want in life if you help enough people get what they want." You need to find some way to lose yourself completely in serving others while doing something you love to do. Your happiness increases as your ability to serve others increases. The harder you work at serving others, the happier you will be. Each day ask yourself this simple question, "How can I increase my service?"

Remember these three unfailing principles:

- ♦   Our rewards in life will always match our service.
- ♦   No one can become rich without enriching others.
- ♦   Anyone who adds to prosperity must prosper in return.

SELECTED THOUGHTS ON SERVICE

The rare individual who unselfishly tries to
serve others has an enormous advantage. He has
little competition. *DALE CARNEGIE*

Aim for service, not success, and success will follow.
B.C. FORBES

I don't know what your destiny will be, but one
thing I know: the only ones among you who will
be really happy are those who have sought and
found how to serve. *ALBERT SCHWEITZER*

Man is here for the sake of other men only. We are
here for the sake of serving others--only!"
ALBERT EINSTEIN

CUSTOMERS

Business exists to serve customers, and unless it does
that, it fails. *WILLIAM FEATHER*

The purpose of any business is to attract and satisfy
people who will become and remain loyal customers.
Customers are the most important element of your
business. Create customers and then treat them as the
most important people on earth. Value their problems.
Make them feel needed and important and you will not
have to worry about your "bottom line."

Successful business people know that you have to work
as hard to keep old customers as you do to attract new
ones. Too often you ignore your existing steady

customers in an attempt to attract new ones. The average business spends about six times more money to attract new customers than it does to keep old ones. That is a big mistake. Companies that work the hardest to serve their customers are the ones you remember. They are the ones you are eager to give your business to over and over again.

♦ ♦ ♦ ♦ ♦

Here is a simple example of how easy it is to treat your customers properly and have them always remember your unusual service. Consider the gas station you usually patronize. If your experience is like mine used to be, you are rarely, if ever thanked, much less thanked by name. You feel ignored and completely taken for granted.

At my service station there is a polite, smiling young man who not only thanks me, but thanks me by name! He also asks me to come back again! Initially, I was so flabbergasted I couldn't wait to go back to see if this seemingly earnest show of appreciation was for real. It was! And this very simple, outstanding attention and service has continued. Now, I am eager to tell everyone about the wonderful, personal service I receive.

♦ ♦ ♦ ♦ ♦

After your customers buy your product or use your service, they feel that they have done you a favor. They feel your business "owes them one." And you do. They deserve to be rewarded with superb continuous service.

Remember, a repeat customer is your most valuable customer.

♦ ♦ ♦ ♦ ♦

No matter how hard you work at customer service, you are certain to have complaints once in a while. Embrace the customers who take the time and trouble to complain. They are your best friends. Those people are doing you two favors:

- ♦ They are pointing out an area where you can improve your business and your service.
- ♦ They are giving you an opportunity to solve their problems and retain them as customers.

All too often dissatisfied customers do not write, call or complain. They simply leave and do not come back. That is their way of saying, "I am fed up and tired of being pushed around. I will take my money and my business elsewhere." Treat customer complaints as marvelous opportunities to find out what you are doing wrong and to correct the problem immediately.

You must constantly evaluate your customer service. Keep asking yourself, "How may we serve our customers better? Are our customer relations improving or deteriorating? Are we fulfilling our promises and our obligations? Are we neglecting anything?" You need to communicate to your customers that you:

- Appreciate their past support.
- Cherish the relationship you have developed.
- Are working very hard to make sure that you will warrant their future confidence.

The purpose of your business is to create and keep customers. You must feel and know deep inside you that your customers are the most important people on earth. Each customer is the lifeblood of your business and an ambassador for your company. The service, care and treatment they receive are a mirror of your business philosophy. Stew Leonard, the supermarket genius, has two rules when it comes to his customers:

- The customer is always right.
- If the customer is ever wrong, go back and read rule number one.

SELECTED THOUGHTS ON CUSTOMERS

The most successful business enterprises today are
the ones that strive first, last, and all the time to
give their customers full value for their money,
to give satisfaction, to please patrons. To
succeed permanently, a firm or corporation must
ask itself squarely: "What is there in it for
those who deal with us?" *B.C. FORBES*

The longer I'm in business, the more I'm convinced
that the real secret of success is our attitude toward
our customer. *STEW LEONARD*

Taking reliable care of your customers is what keeps
them buying, multiplying and coming back. Your
customers will get better when you do.
MICHAEL LEBOEUF

UNCOMMON LEADERS/PEAK PERFORMERS

Leadership is the ability to get other people to
do what they don't want to do and like it.
HARRY TRUMAN

Peak performers in every field are made and not born.
Their success is a matter of nurture, not nature. They
are not necessarily better, smarter or more gifted than
others. They are usually individuals who have made the
necessary effort to develop completely their potential.
Peak performers realize the importance of continuous
self-improvement and take responsibility for their own
growth and maturity. They are thinkers, planners and
doers. You can become just about anything you want
if you are willing to pay the price in terms of hard
work.

The most effective leaders create a sense of esprit de
corps, a spirit that inspires others to much greater
efforts and accomplishments than they would have had
they been left on their own. Uncommon leaders rarely
have to criticize, but when they do, they criticize the
performance, and praise the performer. Their
expectations as an employer have a direct bearing on
their employees' performances. They know that many
people have gone a lot farther in life than they thought
they would because someone else believed in them. As

Galileo said, "You cannot teach a man anything; you can only help him to find it within himself."

Employers generally get the employees they deserve. Employees never complain of discipline if they know it is fair and if they have a hardworking leader who leads by example. People have a tendency to do no more than what is required. The paradox is that the less that is required, the unhappier they become. It is the leader's job to bring out the quality, the excellence and the greatness of the people who have been there all the time waiting to be directed, motivated and inspired. The people will reflect their leadership. The success of the entire organization depends on it.

The attitudes of the people in an organization will always reflect the attitude of the leader. The leader is always one person, the company "parent" who makes the wheels turn. Contrary to popular thinking, you do not raise morale in an organization. Morale filters down from the top.

Effective leaders encourage teamwork which does not happen by accident. Teamwork begins by telling people the organization's philosophy. At our first interview with prospective employees, we clearly define the two essential elements for success in our organization:

♦   You must be a nice person with whom everyone else enjoys working.

- You must adhere to our corporate philosophy: Strive for perfection; settle for excellence.

Uncommon leaders reward teamwork and superior performance in two simple ways:

- Recognition. Recognition costs little or, in many cases, nothing. And almost everyone responds to it. It is amazing how hard people will work when the payoff is appreciation and importance.
- Money. They pay for performance and they get performance.

Uncommon leaders and peak performers have these characteristics:

- They think.
- They relax.
- They visualize and picture themselves performing successfully.
- They go out and create what they have imagined.
- They possess a passionate sense of mission.
- They are obsessed with excellence.
- They are experts in their fields.
- They set specific priorities.
- They give attention to details and have work habits that are systematic and disciplined.

- They are results oriented, not activities focused.
- They have great organizational talents.
- They are compulsive about customer service.
- They trust their own inner signals rather than going along with the group.
- They have faith in people and are willing to collaborate with others.
- They are willing to take risks. They use mistakes as opportunities for growth and self-improvement.
- They act like "they own the place."

SELECTED THOUGHTS ON
LEADERS/PEAK PERFORMERS

To lead people, walk behind them. *LAO-TZU*

The simple virtues of willingness, readiness, alertness and courtesy will carry a young man farther than mere smartness. *HENRY DAVISON*

My grandfather told me that there are two kinds of people; those who do the work and those who take the credit. He told me to try to be in the first group; there was much less competition there.
INDIRA GANDHI

The ideal business temperament would be someone who has a sense of humor, an empathy for people, an understanding of people, and can use his intuitive and innate feelings about people to maximize the business opportunities he's presented with.
MARK H. McCORMACK

234

Always tell yourself: The difference between
running a business and ruining a business is I.
FRANK TYGER

The most important single ingredient in the formula
of success is knowing how to get along with people.
THEODORE ROOSEVELT

I never got far until I stopped imagining I had to
do everything myself. *FRANK W. WOOLWORTH*

I will pay more for the ability to deal with
people than any other ability under the sun.
JOHN D. ROCKEFELLER

A strong leader knows that if he develops his
associates, he will be even stronger.
JAMES F. LINCOLN

People who really achieve greatness make a leap---
they make an imaginative, a creative, a visionary
leap into the future. They create that vision in
their own mind, and then they steer themselves
and their organizations toward that vision.
LAWRENCE M. MILLER

I think the obligation of each one of us is to
leave a legacy, and the most important legacy
that you can leave is a team that is committed,
dedicated, knowledgeable, trained, pointed,
energized and one that works. And that team
doesn't dissipate the minute one person walks out.
PHILIP CALDWELL

The most successful, highest-up executives
carefully select understudies. They don't strive
to do everything themselves. They train and
trust others. This leaves them with time to think.
They have time to receive important callers, to pay
worthwhile visits. They have time for their families.
B.C. FORBES

EDUCATION

Education is that which remains when one has
forgotten everything he learned in school.
ALBERT EINSTEIN

The purpose of education is to help us make the most
of our lives. A good education teaches us, and allows
us, to enjoy and love life for its own sake. Education is
the process of narrowing the gap that exists between
where we are and what we want to become. An
educated person is one who has developed his mind so
that he can obtain anything he wants without violating
the rights of others. He knows where to get the
knowledge he needs and how to organize that
knowledge into definite plans of action.

Successful people never stop learning, never stop
acquiring specialized knowledge in their main area of
interest, profession or business. Unsuccessful people
usually make the mistake of believing that acquiring
knowledge ends when you finish formal schooling. The
formal degrees you earn are necessary. They provide
the pedigrees you need to open doors, to get a job.
Then your real learning begins because formal

education has done precious little to help you acquire the practical knowledge you need for success.

After you have completed your formal education and earned your degree, try to find a mentor. A mentor is a "wise and trusted counselor." A mentor can be a school teacher, a parent, a friend, a manager---anyone who represents what you want to become. A mentor is a very practical person who has experience, has been down the road before, and wants to help you avoid some of the pitfalls.

Does the mentor system work? Consider what is believed to be the greatest intellectual succession in history: Socrates taught Plato; Plato taught Aristotle; and Aristotle taught Alexander the Great. We might not have had the great words of Plato if it had not been for Socrates and his questioning method of teaching. And, the only reason we know anything about Socrates is because Plato wrote down his words. Socrates never wrote down anything.

♦ ♦ ♦ ♦ ♦

A major difference between winners and losers is their attitude toward spending time and money on their own education and self-improvement. Winners realize that they themselves are their most precious asset. Winners are always looking at achieving a higher level of mental fitness and preparedness.

Losers do not believe in themselves and make excuses for not investing time and money in themselves. Most losers are unconscious incompetents. They do not know and do not know they do not know. To them I say, "If you think education is expensive, try ignorance."

◆ ◆ ◆ ◆ ◆

Here are some ideas for self-improvement:

◆   You are your most valuable asset. Personal development is your springboard to excellence and high achievement. You need continuous growth. Do not stop growing. Do not stagnate. Work at least as hard on yourself as you do on your job.

◆   Become curious, interested, open, adjustable, flexible and teachable.

◆   If you want to be successful, study success. Become an expert. Learn proven success methods from others so that you will not have to reinvent the wheel. Attend courses and seminars given by people who have already achieved success. These courses are better than college courses which are often taught by "ivory tower" people who sit and study in theoretical environments but who have very little practical experience. There is no substitute for practical knowledge and practical experience.

♦ Associate with successful people. Learn from them. Emulate them. Winners encourage you to win; losers encourage you to lose.

♦ Increase your productivity. Do you think you could increase your productivity by as little as 2% a month? Of course you can. If you can improve your productivity 2% per month, that becomes 26% compounded annually, 100% improvement in three years; 1,000% improvement in ten years! How can you increase your personal productivity? Here are some simple suggestions:

♦ Cut out television. The average American adult spends three to four hours a night watching the great cultural wasteland. What a colossal waste of time! Certainly, you can find better things to do than be mesmerized by the "boob tube."

♦ Read. Reading is to the mind what exercise is to the body. Your mind, once expanded, can never return to its original shape. The average American adult reads less than one book a year. Fifty-eight percent of Americans never finish a nonfiction book after high school. Reading newspapers, magazines and books is easy and fun. It will pay dividends out of all proportion to the time, effort and cost involved.

♦ Listen to audio cassette tapes in your car or while riding public transportation. The average person drives 15,000 miles per year. That is approximately 1,000 hours per year in the car which you could spend enjoying exciting learning opportunities. Use that valuable time to become better educated and highly motivated.

♦ Improve your ability to use the English language. Your use of language determines your place on our social ladder and to a large extent controls your income. Seventy-five percent of your income depends on your communication skills. They are your most valuable tools when it comes to getting along with people and getting what you want from life. They are an excellent barometer of your knowledge and are the one thing you cannot hide. The minute you open your mouth and speak, you proclaim to the world where you belong on society's pyramid.

♦ Improve your vocabulary. Tests show that more than any other measurable characteristics, knowledge of the exact meaning of a large number of words accompanies outstanding success.

♦ ♦ ♦ ♦ ♦

Knowledge is power. The more you know, the more power and control you can exercise over your life and your future. Work hard to improve yourself. It doesn't take much time, but it does take persistence. One hour per day of study in any subject can make you an authority in three years, a national expert in five years, an international authority in seven years. With wisdom will come kindness, love, understanding and success. It is never too late to begin.

SELECTED THOUGHTS ON EDUCATION

I never let my schooling interfere with my education.
MARK TWAIN

To read without reflecting is like eating without digesting. *EDMUND BURKE*

That which we do not call education is more precious than that which we call so.
RALPH WALDO EMERSON

It is the studying that you do after your school days that really counts. Otherwise, you know only what everyone else knows. *HENRY DOHERTY*

Fifty years ago I knew everything; now I know nothing; education is a progressive discovery of our own ignorance. *WILL DURANT*

We never understand a thing so well, and make it our own, as when we have discovered it for ourselves.
RENE DESCARTES

Education is to teach men not what to think but how to think. *CALVIN COOLIDGE*

The trouble with the world is that the stupid are cocksure and the intelligent full of doubt.
BERTRAND RUSSELL

Perhaps the most valuable result of all education is the ability to make yourself do the thing you have to do when it has to be done, whether you like it or not.
ALDOUS HUXLEY

They know enough who know how to learn.
HENRY ADAMS

Thoroughly to teach another is the best way to learn for yourself. *TRYON EDWARDS*

Knowledge is the antidote to fear.
RALPH WALDO EMERSON

We are all ignorant, only about different things.
WILL ROGERS

Education is an investment in yourself; it brings quality to our life. From a practical standpoint, you cannot compete against the top people unless you are educated. Self-education is only the answer after one has made the most of the formal education available to us through the school system. *JERRY BUSS*

Be properly educated and trained. Know your discipline; be competent; keep current. Become very good at something. *ALLAN COX*

242

Knowledge accumulates in universities because
the freshmen bring a little in and the seniors
take none away. *ACADEMIC SAYING*

K.I.S.S.

Simplify, Simplify, Simplify.
HENRY DAVID THOREAU

The K.I.S.S. principal originally stood for "Keep It
Simple, Stupid." Now, in our more sophisticated,
politically correct society, it stands for "Keep it Short
and Simple" or "Keep It Simple and Sweet."
Whichever definition you like is fine. The point is:
Keep It Simple.

We all have a tendency to over-complicate our lives
and create selected self-induced stress by placing
excessive demands on our time, money, energy, spouse,
children, etc.

We suffer from the "more" syndrome. We want more
money; more, bigger, faster cars; more elaborate
homes; more lavish clothes; more, more, more. Why?
Seemingly, because we insist on complicating what
could otherwise be simpler, happier existences.

Set and keep simple to understand, easy to accomplish
goals. Simplicity means keeping first things first and
not losing sight of our focus, of what is important.
When things get out of control, when life seems overly
complicated and overwhelming, consider the K.I.S.S.
principle: Keep It Short and Simple.

Remember Confucius' philosophy: "Life is really simple, but men insist on making it complicated."

SELECTED THOUGHTS ON K.I.S.S.

In character, in manners, in style, in all things, the supreme excellence is simplicity.
HENRY WADSWORTH LONGFELLOW

Simplicity is making the journey of this life with just baggage enough. *CHARLES DUDLEY WARNER*

The obvious is that which is never seen until someone expresses it simply. *KAHLIL GIBRAN*

The dignity of simplicity. If only more people could learn to keep things simple, straightforward, honest.
EARL NIGHTINGALE

With maturity comes the wish to economize--to be more simple. Maturity is the period when one finds the just measure. *BELA BARTOK*

Life is not complex. The man of fixed, ingrained principles, who has mapped out a straight course, and has the courage and self-control to adhere to it, does not find life complex. Complexities are all of our own making. *B.C. FORBES*

Simple pleasures are the last refuge of the complex.
OSCAR WILDE

Luck

Let him learn a prudence of a higher strain. Let him
learn that everything in nature, even dust and
feathers, go in law and not by luck. What he sows,
he reaps. *RALPH WALDO EMERSON*

Too many people attribute the success of others to luck.
Success and happiness are not matters of luck. They
come from your conscious decision to make success
and happiness your constant companions and to take
them with you everywhere, always.

I have two favorite definitions of "luck."

♦ Luck is what happens when preparedness
meets opportunity.
♦ The harder I work, the luckier I get.

Go out and do each day the very best you can with the
certain knowledge you will start to get "lucky." You
will soon discover that your luck consisted of
painstaking preparation and indefatigable persistence.

Selected Thoughts On Luck

Luck is usually the fruit of intelligent application.
The man who is intent upon making the most of his
opportunities is too busy to bother about luck.
B.C. FORBES

Shallow men believe in luck; wise and strong men in
cause and effect. *RALPH WALDO EMERSON*

Luck is not something you can mention in the presence of self-made men. *E. B. WHITE*

Luck is the residue of design. *BRANCH RICKEY*

Luck is an accident that happens to the competent. *ALBERT M. GREENFIELD.*

To succeed, you have to go out and make your own luck. *EARL NIGHTINGALE*

Life is determined by your own choices, your own will, your own persistence in decisions and not by accidents of fate or luck. *ART LINKLETTER*

I figure you have the same chance of winning the lottery whether you play or not. *FRAN LEBOVITZ*

He worked by day and toiled by night.
He gave up play and some delight.
Dry books he read, new things to learn and
forged ahead. Success to earn. He
plodded on with faith and pluck;
And when he won, men called it luck.
IOWA UNIVERSITY WRESTLING TEAM

Success is not a matter of luck. It is mainly a matter of first, work; second, work; third, work---with, of course, a plentiful mixture of brains, foresight and imagination. *B.C. FORBES*

PARTING THOUGHTS

There are no ordinary moments.

Be yourself.

Achieve your potential.

ABOUT THE AUTHOR

I am not a "real" author, just a dad who wanted to pass along some ideas, thoughts, philosophies and experiences to my two terrific kids, Jennifer, a freshman at Rhodes College and Adam, a sophomore at Shaker Heights High School.

♦ ♦ ♦ ♦ ♦

I have a fabulous, loving, supportive wife. How good is she? Twenty-six years ago, before I got married, my grandfather (who was a very astute judge of women) told me that he was very fond of Sheri, but, there was one thing wrong with her: "She's too good for you!" He was absolutely correct.

♦ ♦ ♦ ♦ ♦

For the past twenty-seven years, I have been in the employee benefits consulting business, enjoying every moment. I am extremely fortunate to have wonderful, loyal clients with whom it is a joy to work.

I work hard, but am not a "Type A" personality. With a reasonably compulsive fetish for organization and preparation, I seem to be able to get things done in an efficient and timely manner using these principles:

- ♦ Do Your Own Thing (From the 60's)
- ♦ K.I.S.S.: "Keep It Simple, Stupid" (From the beginning of time!)
- ♦ Just Do It (From the 90's). My official Ohio automobile license plate is: JS DO IT

♦ ♦ ♦ ♦ ♦

I guess I'm spoiled. I have my own business and can do what I want, when I want. With a "family and fun comes first" attitude, I have been able to follow my passions and do the things I truly love: give my kids both quality and quantity time; go to all their tennis matches; take Adam to a baseball game in every major league park; attend Baseball Fantasy Camp, etc., etc. (One friend told me he would like to be reincarnated as one of my kids!)

♦ ♦ ♦ ♦ ♦

Another friend recently told me: "I love and live your philosophy. You are my role model. You have your priorities straight. You do first things first. You're my hero. I want to be like Ned!"

♦ ♦ ♦ ♦ ♦

If this "About the Author" intrigues you, perhaps you will enjoy my book. I hope so!